SS Leviathan

America's First Superliner

SS Leviathan

America's First Superliner

Brent I. Holt

'But with Fate playing her unpredictable hand, the Vaterland became the keystone of our famous "Bridge of Ships" in World War I. She carried 100,000 troops across the Atlantic to fight the very country that had built her. After the war, under her new name *Leviathan*, the pride of the German ship building art became the flagship of our merchant fleet and the most celebrated passenger liner in history.'
Commodore Herbert Hartley, Captain of the *Leviathan* from 1923-1928.'

First published 2009

The History Press
The Mill, Brimscombe Port
Stroud, Gloucestershire, GL5 2QG
www.thehistorypress.co.uk

© Brent I. Holt, 2009

The right of Brent I. Holt to be identified as the Author of this work has been asserted in accordance with the Copyrights, Designs and Patents Act 1988.

All rights reserved. No part of this book may be reprinted or reproduced or utilised in any form or by any electronic, mechanical or other means, now known or hereafter invented, including photocopying and recording, or in any information storage or retrieval system, without the permission in writing from the Publishers.

British Library Cataloguing in Publication Data.
A catalogue record for this book is available from the British Library.

ISBN 978 0 7524 4763 6

Typesetting and origination by The History Press
Printed in Great Britain

Contents

	Introduction	6
	Acknowledgements	7
one	Building a Leviathan	8
two	The End of the Beginning	21
three	War	24
four	What to do with a Leviathan?	41
five	World's Greatest Ship	63
six	1923 – Back on the Atlantic	70
seven	The Roaring Twenties	99
eight	The Long Twilight	105
Appendix I	*Vaterland/Leviathan* Passenger Carrying Statistics	116
Appendix II	1925/1929/1934 Passenger Statistics Comparison	117
Appendix III	*Leviathan* Speed Data	118
	Bibliography	119

Introduction

The story of the *Leviathan* is a fascinating one. She was a remarkable ship, frequently not given the credit she deserves for her contributions to the US Merchant Marine. Although of German origin, the '*Levi*' was very popular and became a household name across America and other parts of the world. She was one of the greatest passenger vessels of her time. Her interiors were stunning and she was an engineering marvel. After her extensive refit by US Lines in 1923, she was the safest and in this author's humble opinion, the best of the 'Ballin Trio'. She also had an adventurous career that made her seem more like a living thing than a hunk of steel.

I believe the story of the *Leviathan* is one worth telling. I hope you enjoy reading it as much as I did writing it.

Brent I. Holt

Acknowledgements

A book is always a collaborative project. I would like to thank the following people for their contributions: Mark Baber, Dave Boone, Stephen Card, Mark Chirnside, Charles Dragonette, Jim Duckworth, John Emery, Jim Holmes, Nicholas Landiak, J. Kent Layton, Bill Miller, Mark Perry, Les Streater, Richard Turnwald, Mark D. Warren and Paul Wright.

I would also like to thank my mother and father for their support, help and interest throughout this lengthy project.

A particular mention should be made of Mark Chirnside. This book might not be in your hands if it was not for him. He acted above and beyond the call of duty and was very patient with this first time author. Thanks, Mark!

Although I never met him, the late Frank O. Braynard deserves another special mention. His six-volume series on the *Leviathan* is now a collector's item and served as inspiration for this book. His contribution to ocean liner history is incalculable and his memory will live on in his many fine books.

I have done my best to avoid errors in this volume, but human beings can and will make mistakes and I take full responsibility for any errors contained therein. Corrections are welcome.

I have also tried to credit images whenever possible to their owners, but the modern world of the internet has sometimes made that very difficult or impossible. In many cases, the photographer's name has been lost to history. I apologise in advance for anyone who feels they should have been credited for a photo in this book. Please let me know and acknowledgment will be given in the future.

one
Building a Leviathan

The first human being who realised that a simple log could be used as a form of conveyance on the water had little idea of the events they were setting into motion. In time, ancient people would learn to tie logs together and make rafts. Later they hollowed out logs and created canoes. A desire to cross the seemingly endless oceans led to the creation of larger vessels powered by oars and sails. The sailing ship would rule the seas for centuries. But it was the development of the steam engine, and its application to ocean going vessels, that truly began the modern era of quick and easy access to any part of the globe.

As with any human endeavour, the steam engine was built and perfected in fits and starts over many years by numerous people. The first steam-powered water pumps came onto the scene in the late 1600s. The early 1800s saw the first practical steamboats in service on inland waterways of the United States and Great Britain. A modified American sailing ship, the *Savannah*, was the first vessel to cross the Atlantic using a steam engine in 1819. When she approached Liverpool, residents thought the ship was on fire. Although she had only used steam for 20 per cent of the trip, the little steamship had proven that steam power was applicable to the oceans. Eventually, the paddle wheel gave way to the propeller and building material for ships went from wood to iron and then steel. Advances in hull, screw, engine and boiler designs led to larger, faster and more reliable liners. The days of the sailing ship were over. Steam was king.

At the beginning of the twentieth century, a 'race' was in the making. But this was not a competition where people gathered at the track to bet on the latest champion horse. This was a race of technology. As with the space race decades later, the premier nations were building larger and larger ocean liners to carry passengers and mail across the 'Great Pond' – the Atlantic Ocean. From 1907–1914, the race would reach a fever pitch. The German lines: Hamburg-Amerikan (*Hapag*) and North-German Lloyd (NDL); and the British lines: White Star and Cunard, would be the primary participants in this 'friendly' competition. Together, these corporate giants would build some of the most famous ships ever to sail the seas.

The year 1897 was a pivotal one for the ocean liner. The SS *Kaiser Wilhelm Der Grosse* swept away all the speed records that year. With a gross tonnage of 14,439 and at 627ft long, the NDL liner was also the largest ship in the world. She had four funnels, elegantly spaced in pairs with a slight rake to them. In some ways, she was the first of the great superliners. Further German giants followed. In 1899, White Star responded with the lavishly appointed *Oceanic*. Although not a record breaker in terms of speed, she took the title of the world's largest liner and was very popular. Cunard found itself struggling to keep pace in the new era. How could Cunard afford to compete with these new ships as their share of the passenger trade was eroding with each new rival liner?

The help came from an unlikely source. In the United States, railroad empire-builder J.P. Morgan decided to extend his control to the oceans as well as the railways. Morgan was one of the most powerful men in the world. His influence went all the way to the top echelons of the US government. He had created a railroad monopoly and used that power to set uniform rates across the country. Why not extend that to the sea

The keel of the *Vaterland* under construction. (*The Shipbuilder*-Mark D. Warren)

The framing of the hull of the *Vaterland*. (*The Shipbuilder*-Mark D. Warren)

lanes? Morgan created the International Mercantile Marine Company (IMM or IMMCO) and either purchased steamship lines, or worked out operating agreements with them. But the real drama began in 1902 when IMMCO took control of the White Star Line. This caused a huge uproar in Great Britain. Some of it was merely patriotic fever, but others worried that White Star vessels might be taken off the British registry, depriving the military of valuable merchant cruisers and transports in time of war. Cunard took full advantage of this situation and asked the British Government for financial aid to build new ships to compete with the Morgan combine. The Government responded quickly and loaned Cunard a substantial amount of money to build two sisterships that would be the largest and fastest liners in the world. When christened in 1907, the *Lusitania* and *Mauretania* broke all speed records and reclaimed the Blue Riband for their country.

The competition heated up over the next few years. With the backing of IMM, White Star announced plans in 1907 to build three grand vessels that would be the biggest ever and have stunning interiors. They would eventually bear the names *Olympic*, *Titanic* and *Britannic*. Although at 21 knots they would be fast ships, they would not be contenders for the speed record. This had distinct advantages for White Star. Speed requires strict design criteria, such as great length along the waterline, a certain hull shape and a narrow beam. This means the amenities available for the passengers must fit within this constraint. Fuel consumption also increases quite a bit for only a few extra knots of speed. *Olympic* burned about 620 tons of coal per day at 21 knots, whilst the *Lusitania* needed nearly 1,000 tons daily at 25 knots. Reduced speed also permitted greater beam, making it possible for increased public room size. The passenger capacity could also be expanded. The less stringent length-to-beam ratio of slower vessels also contributed to a smoother ride with gentler rolling and pitching. The *Lusitania* Class had a reputation as 'rough rides'. The lack of flare in the bow for the Cunard duo also allowed a considerable amount of water to be pushed into the air when they were underway, leaving the forecastle area quite wet. This was, however, a trait of nearly all ships of that era to some degree.

As the twentieth century dawned, a new era of stiff competition began on the North Atlantic run. NDL had the fast and popular *Kaiser Wilhelm Der Grosse*, *Kronprinz Wilhelm*, *Kaiser Wilhelm II* and

Another view of the framing process. (*The Shipbuilder*-Mark D. Warren)

The *Vaterland* is nearly ready for launch in this image. (*The Shipbuilder*-Mark D. Warren)

The *Vaterland* in her natural element for the first time. (*The Shipbuilder*-Mark D. Warren)

Kronprinzessin Cecilie – the first class of liners with four funnels. In the past, Hapag had stayed out of the costly race for the speed trophy, but this time the company decided to build a record-breaker. She emerged in 1900 as the *Deutschland*. She captured the Blue Riband on her maiden voyage and was initially successful. Unfortunately, the ship also suffered from excessive vibration at service speed. Despite tremendous effort the problem was never solved. In 1911 she was renamed *Victoria Luise* and transferred to cruise service. The quest for speed had cost Hapag dearly. But Hapag Director Robert Ballin had learned his lesson and attention soon turned back to liners of more moderate speed with a strict focus on the size and comfort of the passenger accommodation. The *Amerika* of 1905 and the *Kaiserin Auguste Victoria* of 1906 reflected this return to the philosophy that had worked so well for Hapag in the past.

With the creation of IMMCO, Hapag was vulnerable for takeover by the huge shipping combine. However, in 1903 the ever-wise Ballin worked out an agreement with IMMCO that maintained the independence of Hapag. This cleared the way for Ballin to focus on the operation of the company and the continual threat from its rivals to dethrone the transatlantic giant. The White Star Line's planned trio of ships was a definite threat to Hapag. A response from the German company was inevitable.

With the enthusiastic backing of Ballin, Hapag decided to follow White Star's example. They would build three sisterships to maintain a weekly express service across the Atlantic. The first ship was planned to be called *Europa*, but would instead be christened *Imperator* out of political considerations. After White Star began planning the Olympic Class in late 1907, and rumors spread through the shipping world about the 'monster' ships, Hapag moved forward. Between 1908 and 1910, the design grew on paper. As details of the *Olympic* became known more changes were made. The original conception for ships of 800ft in length, 45,000–50,000 tons and a speed of 20 knots soon gave way to more grandiose plans. Was it a coincidence that the *Imperator* Class would exceed the *Olympic* Class liners in many ways? The revised scheme was for liners of over 50,000 tons, 900+ft long, with a service speed of about 22 knots. This seemed to confirm a response to the competition. Some of the public rooms would be three decks high, in contrast to the one-deck affairs on *Olympic*. Indeed, originally the order for the second and third vessels was placed with Harland and Wolff, giving Hapag access to the firm that designed the *Olympic* and *Titanic*. (The order was later cancelled and all three ships were built by German yards.) Hapag also followed White Star philosophy in building fast ships, but not record breakers. As detailed previously this made better economic sense for the company. The mammoth Hapag liners would dominate the Atlantic in the years just before the First World War. They would also do so in the 1920s, but in a way the German company could have hardly imagined.

On 23 May 1912, Kaiser Wilhelm II, the German Emperor, christened the *Imperator* at the traditional launching ceremony with the crash of a champaign bottle. The hull was then towed to the fitting out berth for completion. For the next year, thousands of workers toiled to complete the liner. The *Imperator*'s statistics were impressive – 909ft long, 98ft wide and a gross tonnage of 52,117. (Gross Tonnage is not weight. It measures the internal space of a ship; 100 cu. ft of space equals 1 ton.) She had a cruising speed of 22½ knots and could carry an outstanding 5,000 passengers when fully loaded.

But there were problems with her design. She was top heavy and had a tendency to list in even the calmest weather. Some nicknamed her the 'Limperator.' Her turbines also had a tendency to overheat on occasion, but Hapag kept this under wraps until time could be found for a refit. Nonetheless, she was very popular with passengers, carrying over 3,000 on her maiden voyage in June 1913. In fact, she transported about 50,000 passengers in her first transatlantic season, an average of over 3,500 per trip. This was an incredible figure for the time period. Ironically, she operated at a loss in her first season – indicating the challenge of running such massive ships on a profit-making basis. She also took the title of world's largest ship from White Star's *Olympic*. But her owners were unsatisfied and had major modifications made to her during her first annual overhaul. Albert Ballin even went so far to describe his beloved liner as a 'first-rate hotel, but a third-rate ship.'

Imperator's three funnels were reduced in height by several feet. Some of her heavier fittings were removed and over 2,000 tons of concrete was added to the double bottom. This improved the situation, but the ship would have stability problems her entire career. The engine issues were also corrected. The entire refurbishment cost Hapag not a single penny as the contract with Vulcan stipulated that the builder would pay the costs of any defects in the ship. This amounted to a cost of about £200,000. The yard barely survived the red ink created by their greatest creation.

With the *Imperator* an overall success, attention turned to her sistership building at the Blohm & Voss shipyards. (Vulcan lost the contract for the last two sisters.) Although the name *Europa* was contemplated for the second ship, she would ultimately be called *Vaterland* ('Fatherland'). The new *Vaterland*, or Hull #212, would incorporate several important design changes from her sister. The most important was the use of split boiler uptakes. Ships before the *Vaterland* had uptakes that carried the smoke from the boilers straight up through the superstructure and to the funnels. This meant that the interior of the vessel had to be designed around the uptakes. It was not possible to simply walk down the middle of the ship. This hindered the layout of the public rooms and gave fits to those responsible for planning the layout of the liner. The split uptakes ran up the sides of the ship, linked beneath the funnels on the uppermost deck and then

Vaterland leaves her builder's yard. (*The Shipbuilder*-Mark D. Warren)

The *Vaterland* looks very impressive in her Hapag livery in this period postcard. Could anyone have imagined at this time that this ship would one day be the pride of US Lines? (Author's collection)

The first class gym. (Author's collection)

exhausted the boiler smoke out of the smokestacks as a conventionally built ship would. At long last, there was a way for interior designers to allow the traveling public to walk down the centre of a liner unobstructed for nearly 400ft. It also had the more practical effect of increasing the fuel bunker capacity of the ship. Unfortunately, it would later be found that the split-uptakes resulted in some structural weakness in the upper hull that would cause a slight problem for the *Vaterland* and the third ship of the class.

A significant difference in the exterior appearance of the *Vaterland* when compared to *Imperator* was in the design of the bridge front. The arrangement of the windows was substantially different and the bridge front was painted a mahogany colour. Elegant scrollwork adorned her bow and stern. Hapag had also learned its lesson with *Imperator* and the new vessel would prove to be much more stable than her sister with hull and superstructure modifications.

As with any ship, construction of the *Vaterland* began with the laying of the keel in September 1911. She was built on an incline so that her hull could be launched into the water when ready. Since the keel was the backbone of the liner, it had to be very strong. Hydraulic riveting was used as much as possible and the double bottom was 5.5ft thick. Three hundred and sixteen frames gave the hull its shape and over 37,000 tons of steel was used in the ship. Expansion joints were built into the superstructure to help dissipate the severe stresses that were created by the forces of the sea on the vessel. She had eleven decks. She would be larger than *Imperator* with an overall length of 950ft, a beam of 100ft and a gross tonnage of 54,282. (The extra length was achieved by adding two more frames into the hull compared to her sister.) Her net tonnage, or the space that generated revenue, was 23,548. The bridge was 87ft above the waterline and the top of the funnels was 146ft above the water. Her loaded displacement tonnage was 62,000 tons. Once again, Hapag would own the largest ship in the world.

The launching ceremony of the *Vaterland* was a sight to behold. All was ready on 3 April 1913 for the momentous occasion. The city of Hamburg was justifiably proud of the leviathan that had grown on the stocks for over a year and a half and it showed. Nearby ships, and the town itself, was dressed in patriotic flags. Under the gaze of thousands, Prince Rupprecht christened the liner with a bottle of champagne that shattered against the stem. Then, hydraulic rams pushed against the hull and the mountain of steel began to move. In barely a minute, the hull was afloat. The *Vaterland* was at last in her natural element. A few minutes later, tugs had taken charge of the liner and began to move her to the fitting-out berth. It would take about a year to turn the nearly empty hull into the largest liner the world had yet seen.

One of the first tasks was to install the huge boilers and engines. The *Vaterland*'s propulsion plant was a marvel of modern engineering. She had four boiler rooms with a total of 46 water-tube boilers with three furnaces each. The water-tube boiler was considered a substantial improvement over the older Scotch fire-tube boiler because it weighed less, had greater safety margins and could be fired up more quickly. The units were coal-fired and required approximately 375 men to shovel the coal into the boilers. The heating surface of the boilers was over 210,000 sq. ft. Incoming water for the boilers was stored in fresh water tanks filled at port and routed to feed water heaters to raise its temperature and improve the steam generating capacity. Salt water was not used in the boilers for the obvious reason that salt would be left behind after it was converted into steam and would require time-consuming removal. Steam was produced at about 235lb psi. The steam was routed to four triple-expansion direct-drive reaction turbine sets powering four propellers. The outer shafts were powered by low-pressure turbines, while a high-pressure turbine turned the port inner shaft and an intermediate-pressure unit controlled the starboard inboard shaft.

There were two modes of operation available from the engines. The first was called 'cruising combination'. The engines would run at full power with revolutions of over 180 per minute. The powerplant operated at maximum efficiency at this setting. The second mode was referred to as 'manoeuvring combination'. The ship was restricted to about 16 knots at 119 revolutions per minute. Although not the most fuel-efficient setting, it did allow a more rapid response time from the engines when they were thrown from ahead to reverse. For reverse power, high-pressure turbines were fitted to the inner shafts and low-pressure turbines to the outer shafts. This arrangement allowed the *Vaterland* to attain about half her designed horsepower when running full astern. Nonetheless, she did have all four screws operating in reverse. This provided advantages when manoeuvring that many other vessels lacked. (The triple-screw *Olympic*, for example, had only the outer propellers available for astern power since the centre propeller did not have a reverse turbine fitted.) After the steam had done its work in the turbines, it was passed through four condensers that cooled it, turned it back into water and sent it back to the boilers. Three evaporators were also available to convert salt water to fresh water when needed. These units together could produce 300 tons of fresh water daily for use in the boilers or for drinking.

Above A corner of the first class smoking room. (Author's collection)

Right A 1914 photo of two ladies, obviously first class, strolling down A-Deck of the *Vaterland*. (Author's collection)

The dummy funnel of the *Vaterland* is captured nicely in this view from 1914. (Author's collection)

Some changes were also made in the shape of the hull below the waterline to increase its hydrodynamic efficiency. Compared to her sister, her horsepower was boosted to a minimum 65,000, providing a cruising speed of about 23 knots. A maximum of just over 100,000hp could be produced by the engines. She consumed about 1,150 tons of coal daily at service speed. Her screws revolved 180 times per minute and were nearly 20ft in diameter. For steering the vessel, the largest rudder ever built was installed. Unlike the *Imperator*, the rudder was completely submerged in the water. It tipped the scales at over 50 tons. A 300hp engine was required to move the rudder. The boiler exhaust was routed through the first two funnels only; the third was installed primarily to balance the ship's profile, also providing ventilation for the engine rooms. Each of the three funnels was 64ft high, 30ft wide and elliptical in shape. They were supported by guy wires and painted in the typical Hapag buff colours.

The electrical systems on the liner were equally as impressive. It had to be powerful enough to supply energy to the equivalent of a small city. The *Vaterland* had an enormous appetite for power. Five turbo generators, supplied with steam from the main boilers, produced electricity for nearly 15,000 lights, elevators, deck operating machinery, heating/ventilation equipment and other necessities for a vessel at sea. Emergency diesel generators were also fitted to provide minimal power in case of a major failure in the turbo generators. Unfortunately, the electrical wiring layout used in many liners would turn out to be a problem in the long run. The electrical cables were attached to the hull and deckhouses for grounding purposes. Over a long period of time, the movement of the ship and the natural expansion and contraction of the steel due to temperature changes would damage the wiring, leaving the ships more and more prone to fires as they aged. The insulation of the wiring also left much to be desired. In addition, a 'one-way' wiring system was used that was considered inferior to 'two-way systems.' More than one German liner would see her career cut short by a fire that left the vessel a burned-out hulk, or at least a fire hazard.

The engines and electrical systems would have been useless without the hard work of the roughly 400-member 'black gang.' Deep in the ship's boiler rooms, these men, frequently covered in coal dust, labored almost constantly to feed the boilers with over 1,000 tons of coal per day. It was not an easy job and took some time to master. They had to make sure the coal was evenly distributed across the grill when the doors to the hungry furnaces opened, working in 100-degree temperatures at times. They worked four-hour duty shifts, with a four-hour break in between. (They were obviously given time to sleep as well.) The heat and light from the open boiler doors and dust created a surreal atmosphere that looked like something out of Dante's *Inferno*. The passengers in the decks above likely gave little thought to the tremendous manual labor going on below them.

For safety from collision at sea, the *Vaterland* was divided into thirteen watertight compartments by twelve transverse bulkheads. Three compartments could be flooded at a minimum without endangering the vessel. In addition, an inner skin was arranged longitudinally throughout the machinery spaces and was about 5ft from the outer hull plates. This was frequently referred to as a double hull. In the boiler rooms the space between the inner and outer hull also served as fuel bunkers with a capacity of nearly 9,000 tons of coal. As was common at the time, many of her watertight doors could be closed with the simple flipping of a switch on the bridge.

With the *Titanic* disaster very much in the public's mind, the *Vaterland* would carry 84 lifeboats, more than enough to evacuate all passengers and crew if necessary. Two of the boats were motorised, something not common in the pre-First World War era. Most of the lifeboat davits were electrically operated and could lower a boat to the water in approximately one minute.

The arrangement of the lifeboats for the *Imperator* Class was also innovative for the time. Since there was insufficient room on the uppermost deck to store all the boats, some of them were placed in special recesses in the aft section of C-Deck. This had the effect of breaking passengers into smaller groups when loading the boats, increasing the efficiency of the evacuation process. It also distributed the weight of the boats across the superstructure more evenly – a very important factor in a design that had proven susceptible to excessive rolling in the first ship of the class.

The anchors of the huge ship were, of course, of impressive proportions. The stem anchor weighed 12 tons and the anchor chains were 900ft long. The port and starboard bow anchors weighed in at 11 tons. There was also a spare 11-ton anchor. A hawse pipe was fitted for a stern anchor, but there is no evidence it was ever used.

The new liner had four separate systems for remaining in contact with land. The first wireless set had a range of several thousand miles and could be used at any point in the voyage. Another could reach stations 400 miles away in daylight and 1,200 miles at night. There was also a backup set powered by batteries. Besides the powerful wireless sets, the *Vaterland* was fitted with the first 'wireless telephone' to go to sea. It allowed voice transmissions instead of only Morse code used with the three other systems. Although the range of the telephone was less than the normal wireless at only 100 miles, it was an important advance in ship-to-shore communication.

A more sophisticated navigational aide called the gyroscopic compass replaced the older magnetic compass. (The *Imperator* was the first vessel to have such a device.) There were two of them on board and they were more accurate than magnetic compasses. Since the steel hull of a ship could interfere with a device that used magnetism to determine the direction of a vessel, the gyroscopic compass was

A Hapag ad for *Imperator*. (Author's collection)

considered to be a superior instrument for safely guiding a passenger liner. Each one cost about $10,000, compared to $50 for the previous magnetic compasses. A 'submarine sounding system' also provided a warning when approaching land so as to avoid a grounding incident.

Another interesting safety feature of the *Vaterland* was a search light installed near the Crow's Nest on the forward mast. Hapag boasted that it had 35,000 candle-light power and could be rotated to face nearly any direction. A lever controlled it from the bridge. It was said it could be seen for 40 miles when lit. What practical use it would have, however, was open to much debate.

To protect against fires, the *Vaterland* was fitted with fireproof doors to isolate passenger areas. These doors could withstand temperatures of up to 1,000 degrees. The walls were coated with a 'special fireproof

Left The lobby to the Social Hall. (Author's collection)

Below The beautiful main dining room. (Author's collection)

material' and three staircases could be sealed off to form a fireproof enclosure and escape route for passengers. Over 450 fire detectors were distributed throughout the ship with 100 hand alarms available. There were also about 800 fire sprinklers and 130 hydrants on deck. The liner even had its own fire department.

With adequate ventilation always a concern for such huge vessels, especially in the boiler rooms, the air intake system could deliver 700,000 cu. ft of fresh air into the liner every hour. This was in an era long before air conditioning as we know it today. At the time there was no practical way to cool the air, only to bring it into the ship and heat it if necessary. There was also an innovation in regards to clearing smoke from the Smoking Room. Christened the 'ozone system', it pumped almost pure oxygen into the room. It is obvious as to why this was important in a facility called the Smoking Room.

For the comfort of her passengers, the *Vaterland* had Frahm 'Anti-Rolling Tanks' installed just above the double bottom. Water flowed back and forth in the tanks and, in theory, reduced rolling in rough seas that caused seasickness in passengers and costly replacement bills for Hapag dishes and cups. In fact, Hapag was so confident of this system, that traditional bilge keels were not fitted to the hull. (Bilge keels are fin-like structures that project from the hull below the waterline to ease the rolling motion of the ship.) The effectiveness, however, of the anti-rolling tanks was debatable and it was not until the development of the fin-stabiliser in the 1940s that a practical method was found to substantially decrease rolling of a ship at sea.

The *Vaterland*'s total passenger capacity was amazing for her day. She could carry 752 in first class, 535 in second class, 850 in third class and 1,772 in steerage. When you added in a crew of about 1,234, the *Vaterland* had a maximum capacity of 5,143 people. With unrestricted immigration still in effect in the US, it was obvious that Hapag intended to transport the lion's share of the lucrative steerage traffic.

First class passengers would be greeted by an interior décor that could easily be described as stunning, perhaps even overpowering. Where British vessels tended to create secluded areas for passengers to socialise, the German giants went in the opposite direction. The *Vaterland*'s public rooms were huge for their day. The split-uptakes allowed for an uninterrupted layout that set the new liner apart from her competitors. The Edwardian Era was well represented in the interior design, with dark wood panelling used in force. White and gold colours were also widely used.

The public rooms in first class surely made its high society occupants feel right at home. Most of the rooms were designed to mirror those of the finest hotels on land. Indeed, one goal was to make the passengers forget they were even on a ship; although rough weather most likely ended any such misconception. First class public rooms included the smoking room, library, social hall, winter garden, gymnasium, tea room, dining saloon, Ritz-Carlton restaurant and swimming bath.

On A-deck, the smoking room offered an impressive view over the bow of the liner through large windows. This typically male-only preserve was decorated with dark panelling and stained glass windows with ancient German designs on them. The fake fireplace could be 'lit' when necessary to add a cozy feeling to the room. Small tables were situated throughout, allowing card games and other social activities to take place. There were also some areas to the sides of the room that provided a small dose of privacy to those who wanted it.

The gymnasium was also located on A-deck. It was typical for the time period. It was a rectangular-shaped room that had all the latest exercise equipment. The decoration was relatively simple, with dark wood panelling on the wall and white on the upper wall and ceiling. A skylight topped off the room.

On B-deck, where most of the first class public facilities were allocated, the library was the first room starting from the forward part of the deck. A glassed-in bookcase adorned one wall. (An open bookcase would have invited a librarian's nightmare in heavy seas when books scattered everywhere.) It also had a fake fireplace of similar type as that in the smoking room.

The next room was the social hall and an impressive sight it was. It was about 75ft long, 56ft wide and had a height of 23ft. The ceiling was glass and metal, giving the whole room a light and happy atmosphere. The sides of the room facing the sea had large windows and oversized paintings. The oak walls were detailed with rich carvings in the Louis XVI style. Numerous tables and chairs invited passengers to mingle with old friends and new acquaintances. The room was simply stunning in nearly all respects.

After passing through the lobby, the winter garden (also called the palm court) was the next feature designed to wow the rich and famous. It was filled with flowers and plants and had an elevated section in the middle of the room. Large windows allowed as much light in as was possible on the sometimes gloomy north Atlantic.

Right Another view of the first class library. (Author's collection)

Below A wide view of the Ritz-Carlton Restaurant. (Author's collection)

Above The Winter Garden led into the main portion of the Ritz-Carlton Restaurant. (Author's collection)

The Social Hall was one of the most palatial public rooms on the *Leviathan* and her sisters. (Author's collection)

Left A corner of the Winter Garden. (Author's collection)

One of the most noteworthy sections of first class was the Ritz-Carlton restaurant. It was a nearly exact copy of the restaurant in New York City. It was intended to draw the wealthiest passengers and an extra fee was charged for its use. The room itself could only be described as magnificent, with huge windows, Doric columns and a highly detailed dome to cap off the design.

Rounding out the first class rooms on B-deck was the small tea room. Passengers could take part in a time-honored tradition and then go outside and crawl under a blanket in a deckchair to enjoy the hopefully good weather. At night a spectacular view of the stars could be seen away from the light pollution of the big cities.

The dining room was located on F-deck near the centre of the ship. This provided the best protection to the passengers from the rolling and pitching of the vessel at sea. The room was 100ft across and two decks high. The area of the floor was 11,550 sq. ft. There was also a balcony on E-deck that surrounded the upper portion of the room, from which orchestra played tasteful music. Passengers could make a grand entrance using a staircase that descended into the saloon from the level above. Those seeking a quieter entry could use doors at the forward section of the room. About 700 people could be seated at once, with tables holding from two to eight people. There were even two private dining areas available for passengers. White pillars flanked the room and a huge mural was mounted on the ceiling dome. The dome was 31ft above the floor at the highest point. What a fantastic experience it must have been to dine in such a room!

The stores necessary for the kitchens required organisation on a massive scale. Over 50,000lb of meat; 48,000 eggs; 150,000lb of vegetables; 7,000 quarts of milk; 1,500 ice-cream boxes; over 17,000 bottles of wine; 400lb of chocolate; and 33,000L of beer were stowed aboard for the passengers and crew.

Also on F-deck, the swimming pool for first class was arguably one of the most outstanding rooms of its type ever installed in a liner. With the balcony, it rose through three decks. Doric style columns were at the side of the pool. Its maximum depth was about 8ft and it was filled with saltwater. Pumps could fill the pool with 120 tons of water in 25 minutes. The whole facility harked back to the days of Ancient Rome.

The first class cabins, of course, were of the highest calibre. The door to each had a brass knocker with the room number and a slot for a card to be placed that identified the temporary inhabitants. All rooms had electric lighting and fresh water taps. Only the more expensive cabins had bathrooms, however. Most passengers, regardless of class, were expected to use public facilities. The stewards could be called by the simple press of a button. The heating and air flow from the ventilators could be controlled from each individual cabin. The rooms were decorated in a variety of styles, with colour paintings on the walls. The average first class cabin had about 170 sq. ft of space.

For the richest first class travellers, there were two deluxe cabins called the 'Kaiser Suites' on C-deck. These cabins were divided into nine rooms with 247sq. ft of 'living space'. There were two bedrooms, two bathrooms, a dining area, a room for luggage and even a private promenade in each. The *Vaterland* certainly offered almost anything even the most demanding passengers could desire.

Although close to 75 per cent of the liner's passenger space was devoted to first class, other classes of passengers would not be ignored in the new ship. A smoking room, lounge, restaurant and gymnasium were some of the main public facilities in second class. Third class had much less, with only a smoking room, lounge and dining saloon provided. The domain of the immigrant, steerage, had to be content with three rooms even smaller than in third class. The interiors were very plain at this level and strictly functional. But there was nothing unusual in this arrangement in the years before the First World War, except the huge passenger capacity of the *Vaterland*. She was a ship very much of her time, scaled up to squash the competition in every way possible.

On 29 April 1914, the new liner eased away from her builder's yard for the first time under her own power. Large crowds gathered to watch the mammoth ship leave her birthplace. The letters on both sides of the bow proudly spelled out *Vaterland* with 18in-high brass letters attached to the hull. (The stern letters were 1ft in height.) Her official yard trials were underway. Ahead of her was a career of tremendous excitement and many letdowns. To some, she would be known as the greatest liner ever to sail the Atlantic; others would call her a waste of taxpayer's money in her latter years and a 'white elephant'. It would be a glorious journey, however, and one for the history books.

The *Kaiser Wilhelm Der Grosse* of 1897 is considered by many to be the first of the superliners. (Author's collection)

This postcard of the *Vaterland* was posted in June 1914. (Author's collection)

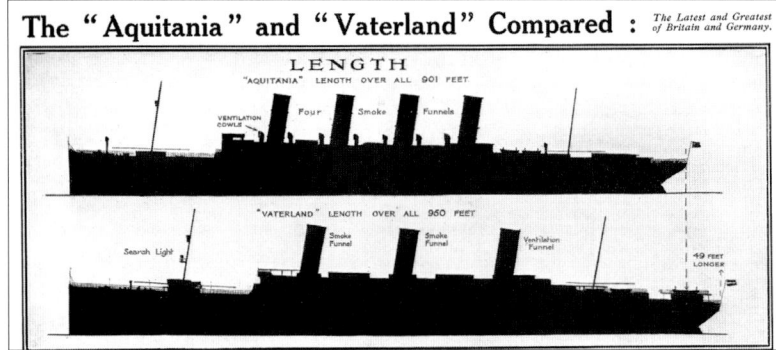

This illustration compares the *Aquitania* and *Vaterland*; both entered service in 1914. (Author's collection)

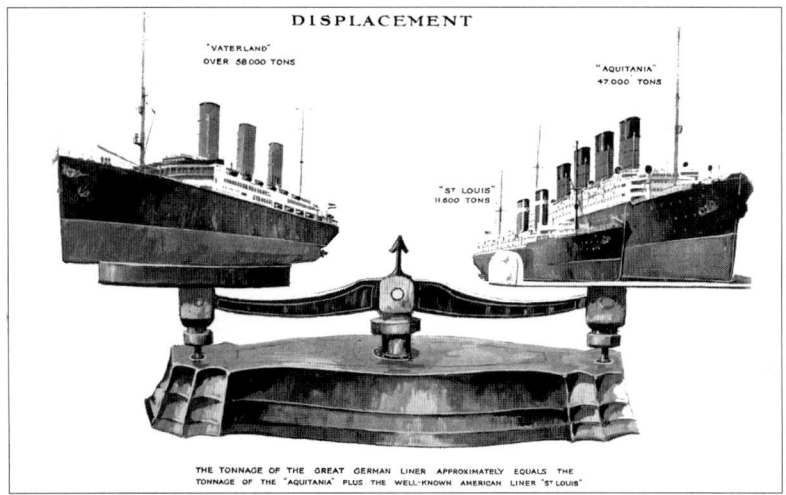

Above A postcard of *Vaterland* in her days as the flagship of Hapag. (Author's collection)

Left This interesting diagram demonstrates the larger size of the new *Vaterland* compared to the American Line's *St Louis* and the *Aquitania* of Cunard. (Authot's collection)

two

The End of the Beginning

At long last, the *Vaterland* was at sea. For the next two days, the ship was put through her paces. She conducted manoeuvring tests and her engine performance was closely scrutinised. She averaged 25.84 knots and briefly reached a commendable 26.3 knots. The engines developed over 90,000hp during the trials. To the relief of all involved, she proved to be a good 'sea boat' with none of the excessive rolling problems of her sister. With the tests successful, Hapag took official delivery of their new ship and preparations for the maiden voyage began in earnest.

On 14 May 1914, the *Vaterland* set sail on her first voyage with paying passengers. It was a dreary, rainy Thursday and only occasionally did the sun peek out from behind the clouds. But the weather did not deter thousands from seeing her off. Under the careful guide of tugboats, the monster ship slowly moved away from the pier. On the bridge, Commodore Ruser supervised the departure and prepared to take his ship to sea. He had eleven deck officers under his command. There were about 1,000 passengers on board, with more to come at Southampton and Cherbourg. About 1,200 crew members accompanied them.

The *Vaterland* arrived at Southampton on Friday. Two small tenders brought more passengers out to her. She then headed for Cherbourg, the final stop before the real journey across the 'Great Pond' began. She reached the French port in the afternoon and set sail in the evening. She had 270 aboard in first class, 142 in second, 355 in third and 910 passengers in steerage for a total of 1,677 people. It was a decent showing for a maiden voyage since some avoided them for superstitious reasons; the *Titanic* was still a very recent memory.

Others felt that it would take a while for a new liner to 'settle in' and preferred to wait until the ship and crew had more experience.

There were several notable people aboard the first crossing. Four high-ranking Hapag officials enjoyed their creation and accepted praise from countless passengers about the new ship. Dr George Brandes, a Danish literary critic, spoke to a *New York Times* reporter about his favorite American poets and said he planned to stay in the US for about three weeks. Another person on the passenger list who drew attention was Paul Rainey, a big-game hunter who was returning from an expedition of over a year in Africa. He boasted about killing a lion and that he had taken over 5,000ft of pictures. (A friend of his was also killed by a lion during a hunt.) Bernard Kellerman, author of the book *The Tunnel*, spent much of the trip watching the engines operate. He said the engines were the part of the liner that was 'alive' and were more interesting than the ship's palatial interiors which he could see in any fancy hotel.

One of the *Vaterland*'s designers, Dr Ernst Foerster, talked to the press about the many advances in design the vessel possessed. He was obviously quite proud of the *Vaterland*. He attributed the higher service speed of the second liner of the class to finer hull lines and increased engine horsepower. The engineer said that any other liners in the near future would likely only be slightly bigger in length and tonnage. Foerster believed that the *Vaterland* and her forthcoming sister probably represented the largest passenger ships to be built for many years because of limits in harbour depths and docking facilities. He pointed out that the third *Imperator* Class liner, the *Bismarck*, would be only a few feet longer than the *Vaterland*. History would prove him right since the *Bismarck/Majestic* would not be exceeded in tonnage until the debut of the *Normandie* in 1935. Also on board was German Admiral Oscar van Truppel and Hermann Frahm, the designer of the anti-rolling tanks fitted on *Imperator* and *Vaterland*. Another notable passenger was Alexander Carlisle. He was a retired ship designer from the famous Harland & Wolff shipyards and one of the chief architects of the *Olympic* and *Titanic*. Now he was aboard a liner that was conceived as a response to the *Olympic* – a vessel he designed! He called the *Vaterland* the most wonderful ship afloat and said that she would remain so for a very long time.

The maiden crossing of the world's largest liner attracted attention from all over the globe. To the relief of Hapag, all went relatively smoothly. The *Vaterland* encountered rough seas that left many seasick. But this was hardly uncommon for the time; or any time for that matter. Another interesting event was a course change necessitated by a report from the US Coast Guard of icebergs in the vicinity. Commodore Ruser stayed on the bridge all night in case his expertise was needed to avoid an iceberg. Fortunately, this proved unnecessary. But after the *Titanic* disaster only two years earlier, it was a prudent move on the master's part.

Overall, the passengers seemed very pleased with the size and sea qualities of the new liner. A group of first class gentlemen sent a congratulatory telegram to Albert Ballin of Hapag that said in part:

> Heartiest congratulations on the successful maiden trip of the *Vaterland*-the greatest as it is the best ship afloat-a monument to your company's intelligent direction, its courage, and its enterprise. The *Vaterland* is a veritable palace afloat and its colossal proportions, ample accommodations, and superb comforts are only surpassed by the sense of safety and security that in every direction impresses the intelligent observer. The happy and satisfied first voyagers on the *Vaterland* send you greetings and felicitations and wish you and your company continued and increasing prosperity.

From Cherbourg to the Sandy Hook Lightship, the *Vaterland* covered 3,177 miles. The crossing was completed at an average speed of 23.2 knots in five days and 17 hours. The most mileage she made in one day was 592. This was a good showing for a new ship. Her ever hungry boilers had consumed about 1,160 tons of coal per day. Her average speeds would increase as the engines 'settled in.' Her draught was about 36ft on her arrival at her US port. The main channel in the Hudson River was only 40ft deep, leaving little clearance for the ship's keel.

The welcome in New York was one of the largest ever for an ocean liner. But before she could dock, the harbour pilot had to come aboard to guide her into port on the final stage of the journey. This turned out to be easier said than done. The *Vaterland* approached the pilot boat at a rather quicker pace than expected. Only the experience of those on the small boat allowed Pilot McCarthy to be in the proper place and time to grab the rope ladder and haul himself aboard the giant of the sea. After a stop at Quarantine for the usual inspection and paperwork, the *Vaterland* at last made her way toward her pier at about 8.30a.m. Another problem developed when the ship was virtually surrounded by a fleet of small boats filled with curious sightseers. Careful manoeuvring was necessary so as not to run over any of them. When it appeared that the liner would at last arrive at her pier, a Leigh Valley Railroad tugboat pulling lighters behind it delayed the ship when it crossed nearly in front of her. Then a strong wind and tide stranded the tug and her cargo in the *Vaterland*'s docking area. All this forced Commodore Ruser to back his ship down the river and wait it out while another tug was called to rescue the other tugboat. Nearly 3,000 people waited for the big ship to dock.

There was more drama as the great ship backed down the river, nearly colliding with a ferry. Only the quick action of the pilot avoided a collision. The big ship also nearly sucked a tug underneath the stern and into the screws when the little vessel got too close. The *Vaterland* then turned and took a position that blocked major river traffic for a half an hour.

At long last, the *Vaterland* found an opening in the wind and tide and headed for Pier 2 in Hoboken. Five hours late, she tied up at 1.15p.m. The

The new *Vaterland* at sea. (Author's collection)

excitement was over. The first crossing had been completed successfully. Her departure five days later would surely be a quieter affair?

After her first passengers had disembarked, the task of 'turning the ship around' began. The liner had to take on supplies and be thoroughly cleaned before the next crossing. The ship needed almost constant painting since rust appears very quickly on a vessel sailing in salt water. Fuel also had to be taken on board. Coal elevators were nestled alongside the liner and dumped over 8,500 tons of coal into the bunkers in just under a day. This was a messy job. Coal dust always seemed to find its way into the passenger areas and required cleaning up.

At last, the *Vaterland* was ready for the return leg of her maiden voyage on 26 May. There were 2,307 passengers aboard in all classes. What happened next is still not completely understood. All of a sudden the gigantic liner burst out of her pier and headed across the Hudson for the shore. Two tugs tried to stop her mad dash, but they could do little. It is possible that there was a malfunction of some type. Perhaps Captain Ruser signaled full forward to get the liner moving out of her pier and then the changeover valves did not redirect the steam to the forward turbines when called for? Regardless of the reason, the *Vaterland* wreaked havoc on river shipping. A coal barge was sunk and the backwash damaged other lighters and the pier itself when they were pushed against it by the force of the water. Two small liners broke free of their moorings. One man died when he was washed off his small boat. The engines were likely ordered full ahead and after some time they responded. The big ship stopped just in time and it was a very close call. The incident was front page news. Hapag could have done without that type of publicity, however. It is likely that the *Vaterland*'s astern turbines were damaged during the frantic effort to stop the charge across the river.

Overall, the last leg of the maiden voyage was uneventful. On 30 May, the brand new Cunarder *Aquitania* passed the *Vaterland* at night. It seemed as if every light aboard her was turned on. Her four colorful funnels must have looked impressive. It was quite a sight. The *Vaterland* completed the trip on 1 June. The average speed for the first voyage (two crossings) had been 22.4 knots.

The competition on the North Atlantic was tremendous in the summer of 1914. Not only did Hapag have to contend with the *Aquitania*, but the *Lusitania* and *Mauretania* from Cunard as well. Cunard operated a three-ship express service with these three giants that could not be ignored. White Star had the very popular *Olympic* and *Britannic* was expected to be completed by autumn. The French Line's *France* had also carved an enviable reputation for herself.

But Hapag had little to worry about in reality. The *Imperator* and *Vaterland* were doing extremely well. The *Vaterland* would finish out the season as the second most popular liner in service, eclipsed only by her elder sister. The *Aquitania* would finish a distant third. The public had spoken: Hapag had the greatest liners on the Atlantic. With the 20 June launching of the *Bismarck*, the company could soon look forward to having the ultimate three ship express service. It seemed that nothing could get in the way of boundless prosperity in the future for the German merchant marine. The best was yet to come.

But world events were conspiring to end the dream of Hapag. On 28 June 1914 Archduke Ferdinand of Austria was assassinated by a Serbian national. The administration of Austria, suspecting that the Serbian government was behind the shooting, sent a series of demands to Serbia. Serbia refused to accede to all the demands. A series of alliances between several major nations rapidly led to the outbreak of the Great War in August 1914, one of the most destructive conflicts in world history. Great Britain, Russia and France (the Allied Powers) joined forces to face the might of the German and Austrian military (the Central Powers). Eventually, 65 million soldiers from 35 countries served in the war.

The coming of the First World War brought the transatlantic passenger trade to a sudden halt. It was now too dangerous to risk crossing an ocean infested with U-boats. The *Vaterland* had made seven crossings of the Atlantic before war clouds forced Hapag to cancel the return portion of her fourth voyage, scheduled to leave on 1 August. About 2,700 people had booked the passage and the loss to Hapag was estimated to be in the region of $225,000. Hapag released a statement to the press:

> In view of the uncertainty of the present European situation we have decided to postpone the sailing of the *Vaterland* tomorrow…Due notice will be given of the eventual sailing date.

The last sentence turned out to be an overly optimistic one. Many thought the war would be over very quickly but they were wrong. The *Imperator*'s 31 July sailing from Germany had been cancelled and she would sit out the war in Hamburg. The *Vaterland* would do the same, but on the other side of the Atlantic. Who could have known that the two sisterships would never again sail under the Hapag flag? The first phase of their lives was over. A new and uncertain future awaited them.

three

War

As the war raged on, the *Vaterland* remained laid-up at Pier 4. Nearly half of her crew went home in the weeks that followed the cancellation of the ship's sailing schedule. Commodore Ruser's wife and son even journeyed to the US to be with him. Minimal maintenance procedures and a regular watch was kept. It was an odd point in time for the world's largest vessel. She was designed to brave the North Atlantic; now she was the virtual social centre for Germans in the New York area.

On 7 May 1915 the *Lusitania* was sent to the bottom of the ocean by a German submarine. The *Lusitania* was one of the few liners to remain in commercial service during the war. She took 1,198 lives with her, including 124 Americans. This act was unprecedented in modern combat. The Cunarder was not employed by the British Admiralty; her unprovoked sinking changed the course of warfare. If a passenger vessel could be sunk with impunity, then what rules were left in war? The *Lusitania* tragedy virtually ended any chance that America might eventually side with Germany in the First World War. The stage had been set for the US to enter the fighting on the side of the Allies.

Relations between the United States and Germany only worsened over the next two years. The Germans, with the war turning against them, announced that they would destroy nearly any ship they pleased on 1 February 1917. They even demanded that American vessels paint their hulls with red and white stripes to avoid attack. Then word spread that Germany had promised to give Mexico a portion of their former territory in the US if they would attack the nation. This was the final straw. On 6 April, the Congress of the United States declared war on Germany. The full power of the massive industrial capacity of the US would now be on the side of the Allied Powers. The German liners in American ports were quickly eyed for seizure. The *Vaterland*'s days under the flag of the Fatherland were numbered.

It all happened very quickly. On the day war was declared federal agents, with 200 troops, boarded and seized control of 91 German vessels. When the *Vaterland* was captured the officer on watch simply said 'I protest.' The remaining crew members were removed and some accepted US citizenship. The rest were interned.

With the stars and stripes now flying at her stern the *Vaterland* was far and away the biggest ship in the American merchant fleet. At the suggestion of President Wilson, the liner was given a new name: *Leviathan*, a suitable choice for such a huge vessel. Plans were made to convert the *Leviathan* into a troop transport. It was soon discovered, however, that several problems had to be solved before this could become reality.

The US had never operated a vessel of the *Leviathan*'s size. There was much to learn in order to run her at peak efficiency. Her size enabled her to carry an enormous amount of troops and make a substantial contribution to the war effort. But her dimensions also caused headaches. New York port facilities could barely accommodate her, not to mention docks overseas. The ship drew up to 40ft of water and Ambrose Channel could just accommodate her. The channel was dredged to 40ft in low water conditions, but spring tides could reduce this to 39ft. Strong currents and winds could also worsen the situation. Careful timing was required to get the *Leviathan* out of Hoboken without running aground. Fourteen to sixteen tugboats would be needed to assist her departures.

The *Leviathan* had been idle at her pier for nearly three years. Barnacles were encrusted all over the hull below the waterline and silt had built up to the point that the ship was stuck in the mud. The departing German crew had also destroyed the blueprints and other documents that would have been helpful in preparing the liner for her new duties. Mechanically the *Leviathan* also needed work. Her astern turbines were found to be inoperative – a likely result of her accidental race across the Hudson when she departed for her second Atlantic crossing. Obviously Hapag had not repaired the turbines and the problem had only gotten worse on her subsequent trips. Many of the boilers had not been fired up for some time as well. Apparent sabotage was discovered when floods were caused after the water was turned on in the ship. Further investigation revealed cut and bent pipes behind the bulkheads. It would take some doing to get the big ship up and running again.

In June 1917 the *Leviathan* was transferred to the control of the Navy. The turbines and boilers were repaired, divers cleaned the ship's hull as best they could, dredgers were called in to remove the silt from underneath the ship so she could leave when called upon, bunks for over 7,000 troops were installed and the liner was given a thorough cleaning inside and out. By the end of July the *Leviathan* was officially commissioned and over 2,300 crew members began to come on board.

Above A wartime view of one of the USS *Leviathan*'s funnels. (Author's collection)

Left Troops aboard USS *Leviathan*. (Author's collection)

The USS Leviathan in dazzle paint. (Author's collection)

This dramatic photograph of the USS Leviathan from the Great Northern emphasises the rough sea and how even huge ships were at the mercy of Mother Nature. (Author's collection)

USS Leviathan in somber gray paint. (Author's collection)

More modifications were made over the next several months. She was fitted with two 30-calibre machine-guns and eight 6-inch guns. Two 1-pdr cannons were placed on C-deck in September 1918. A depth charge launcher was also installed on the stern for submarine defence. A cargo hold was transformed into a storage centre for munitions. Her hull was painted a simple, sombre, grey. The mooring trials of her engines were conducted on 12 November 1917, with the shafts disengaged from the turbines. At last, all seemed ready.

On 17 November 1917 the *Leviathan* backed out of Pier 4 for the first time in 3½ years for her second round of trials since she was completed in 1914. She was going back to sea again. In addition to her regular crew there were 241 relief marines on board for transfer to Guantanamo Bay, Cuba. She initially took an easterly course to confuse spectators as to her actual destination, but later turned southward towards Cuba and warmer waters. The captain posted the marines in highly visible positions to give the impression the liner was filled with troops. As the *Leviathan* steamed southward, the crew painted the glass in the portholes and windows black to avoid enemy detection. All sources of light, even matches, were forbidden to be visible outside the ship. The crew was also told not to throw anything overboard since this could leave a trail for subs to follow. In the days before sonar and radar, these were the best methods to reduce the risk of being spotted by a German submarine. The possibility of a U-boat attack was taken very seriously.

The trials were not without problems, however. The steering gear was disabled on several occasions and the ship rendered helpless. The *Leviathan* had to stop more than once. Eventually the mechanical department devised a permanent fix, but it left the crew in a nervous mood. Luckily the failure had not occurred in the submarine infested North Atlantic shipping lanes.

The great liner finally arrived at Guantanamo Bay and dropped anchor. Her draft was too deep to tie up directly at the dock so tenders removed her marines and brought aboard those bound for home. The crew fished for sharks while waiting for the troop transfer to be completed. With her trials finished, the *Leviathan* returned to Hoboken. She was at last deemed ready to take up her role as a troop transport.

With over 7,200 troops on board, the *Leviathan* left New York on 15 December 1917 with the assistance of twelve tugboats. She was bound for Liverpool and a long overdue dry-docking. There was not a

"LEVIATHAN"

(Author Unknown)

Leviathan, thou noble ship,
Thou mighty monarch of the seas,
May thy stalwart form and mighty force
War's desolating horrors ease.
We view the grandeur of thy bulk,
And gaze with wonder and with awe
At thy great magnitude and might
Which surpass visions we foresaw.

As now in peaceful anchor held,
The waves caress thy sturdy bow:
The ocean flirts and beckons thee
To sail away, away—and now
She lures thee with her shining crest,
But couldst thou see beneath the wave
The yawning jaws of cavern greed
From which a God alone can save.

She'll lure thee out into her midst,
Then tantalize with storm and gale,
But these mere trifles bring no fear
As ever on you sail.
But deep within her somber soul
There lie devices born of hate,
In traitorous hearts and crafty minds
Hell's strategies they propagate.

And will these mechanisms harm?
Will bomb or shot e'er rend thy bark?
Will cries of horrors fill the air
As dangers peer from ocean dark?
There is but One who knows thy fate;
Within the hollow of His hand
Thy safety lies. You can but wait
And place thy trust in Beulah Land.

We trust thee, ship, we give our sons
By thousands. Will they fill thy halls?
Oh bring them safe across the wave
Despite the whirlpool, storms and squalls.
The prayers and sobs from broken hearts
Will follow as thy course is run.
This prayer eternal, to heaven will rise—
"Thy will, not mine, Oh, God, be done."

Leviathan, thou ship of state,
Sail on, sail on victorious.
Crush thou the tools of hate,
Come back with honors glorious
And bring with thee eternal peace.
Peace with honor, without stain,
And wear the crown *"LEVIATHAN,"*
Queen of the ocean's vast domain.

A poem about the *Levi*. (Author's collection)

dry-dock in the US large enough to hold her. A heavy snow was falling on departure. The crossing was not an easy one, rough weather left more than one passenger seasick. She worked her speed up to 21½ knots when the sea conditions permitted. Gun drills took place and the crew repeated abandon ship procedures daily. A 'zigzag' course was practiced to avoid U-boats. On 23 December, another event scared many troops to death. All of a sudden, in the middle of the ocean, the ship's whistles moaned across the empty water. In the deep sea this was considered an emergency signal and many scrambled for their boat stations and feared the worst. As it turned out, it was a malfunction caused by the low temperatures forcing the wire to the whistles to contract. This would not be the last time this would happen. An escort of US destroyers joined the *Leviathan* for the final part of the crossing.

Unfortunately, inferior quality coal prevented her from averaging her usual 22–23 knots the whole trip and she arrived behind schedule on 24 December. It took some time to tie up at the floating Princess Landing Stage and disembark the soldiers. Then the giantess simply

Troops prepare to disembark the USS *Leviathan* at NYC. (Author's collection)

Food preparation for thousands of troops. (Author's collection)

The boiler room of the USS *Leviathan*. Temperatures here reached over 100 degrees during the days of coal-fired boilers. (Author's collection)

Sleeping areas for troops aboard USS *Leviathan*. (Author's collection)

The turbine controls. (Author's collection)

The Winter Garden and Ritz Carlton were used to feed troops in addition to the regular facilities. (Author's collection)

Troops also slept on the Promenade Deck. This can't have been comfortable in rough weather! (Author's collection)

waited for the right tide conditions to enter the Gladstone dry dock. There were only two days a month that conditions were acceptable. Her deep draft meant there were very few facilities in the world that could handle her properly and it took nearly three weeks before the tides cooperated. In the meantime careful preparations had to be made. Working without any docking plans, keel blocks were carefully placed in the dock so the ship would not unduly strain herself once the water was pumped out. The first attempt on 14 January 1918 failed when high winds made it impossible to proceed. The next day would be more successful. Using her own engines, the *Leviathan* was carefully guided into the graving dock under the guidance of a Cunard Line officer. The water was pumped out slowly over a three-day period. The pumps were stopped frequently so that divers could verify that the hull was settling properly on the keel blocks. Over the next month her hull and screws were scraped and cleaned and everything below the waterline was carefully inspected and repaired if needed. Modifications were made to accommodate an additional 1,000 troops. A paravane system was installed at the bow of the ship to intercept mines before they contacted the hull. She was also given a fresh coat of paint that substantially altered her appearance.

USS *Leviathan*. (Author's collection)

More images of USS *Leviathan*. (Author's collection)

USS *Leviathan* in the Gladstone Drydock in Liverpool. (Author's collection)

Commanders of the USS *Leviathan* during her trooping duties. (Author's collection)

Over 1,000 orphans were treated to a Christmas they would never forget on the USS *Leviathan* in 1918. (Author's collection)

Orphans pose with Father Christmas aboard the *Levi* in 1918. (Author's collection)

USS *Leviathan* in the Gladstone Drydock in Liverpool. (Author's collection)

Officers of USS *Leviathan*. (Author's collection)

An officer uses a sextant on deck. (Author's collection)

Engineering officers of USS *Leviathan*. (Author's collection)

Navigators and physicians of USS *Leviathan*. (Author's collection)

It was called 'dazzle paint' and consisted of colorful geometric shapes and lines painted onto the ship. Although it might seem foolhardy to paint a military transport in bright colours, there was a strategy behind it. The goal was not to make the vessel invisible, but to make it difficult to recognise and, more importantly, hard to target. The scheme could make it appear that the liner was going in another direction or on a different heading. It was used widely in the First World War, but not as much in the Second World War. Its effectiveness is still debated.

The debate aside, it certainly gave what could be an otherwise drab troopship a lively appearance.

The crew of the *Leviathan* was granted leave in Liverpool at certain times. Some, of course, sneaked off the ship when they could. To try to keep them out of trouble, a '*Leviathan* Patrol' was established in which officers would walk the street and attempt to minimise any problems that might result from the presence of the crew in Liverpool. The patrol was split into four groups and one was even sent to the local

Nurses aboard the troop transport *Leviathan*. (Author's collection)

however, an escorting destroyer suddenly opened fire on an object about 250ft away. The *Leviathan* herself shook from the detonations and some on board thought the ship had struck a mine. The identity of the suspicious object was never determined.

After the normal disembarking of troops, the *Leviathan* once again was placed into the Gladstone dry dock for minor hull work. The stay in Liverpool was a little under a month. The liner left the British port on 10 April and headed for the US once again. She had some unusual passengers on this trip: German POWs. There were 33 enlisted soldiers and four officers among the prisoners. The officers were given cabins on C-deck while the enlisted men had to make do with sitting in the police station. Overall, things went smoothly. There was a complaint, however, that the Americans' shoes made strange noises. This turned out to be caused by coins in their shoes. Most sailors had little pocket space and so they tended to put their coins into their socks. The coins eventually worked their way to the shoes and inspired the nickname 'clackers' for the money.

On 9 February 1918 the *Leviathan* sailed for home. Any hopes of the second crossing being smoother than the first were quickly dashed when a severe storm was encountered. Giant waves smashed against the ship, causing much damage. Then thick fog forced the liner to slow down around the Grand Banks for eight hours. Still in thick fog, the liner docked at Pier 4 on the morning of 19 February. Voyage 1 of the USS *Leviathan* had been completed.

While the *Leviathan* was being turned around in port, it was decided to increase her troop capacity yet again. As experience was gained operating the mammoth vessel, it became obvious that with the proper organisation she could carry many more troops than originally intended. An additional 650 bunks were installed, raising her troop carrying capabilities to just under 9,000.

The *Leviathan* began her second voyage as a troop carrier on 4 March 1918. On board were over 8,200 troops. The crossing was relatively uneventful, with generally good weather. Towards the end of the trip,

The bridge of USS *Leviathan* and the ship's band. (Author's collection)

brig. The officers were allowed to eat dinner, under guard, in the Ritz-Carlton restaurant. Many of the ship's crew took great pleasure in pointing out to the Germans that they were aboard a captured Hapag vessel. When asked about lifeboat arrangements, the officers were told that they could expect the same treatment that their comrades had provided for the passengers of the sunken *Lusitania*. Luckily for them, lifeboats would not be needed on this crossing. On 17 April, the *Leviathan* returned to her berth in Hoboken. The prisoners were transferred to a holding facility in Georgia.

At this stage in the *Leviathan*'s troop carrying career, a problem became obvious: it was taking her too long to turnaround between crossings. She had completed only two voyages in a four-month period, with a mean turnaround time of 54 days. And of these, only two crossings carried troops. This was hardly the best way to use such a large vessel to maximum advantage for the Allies. The primary reason for the delays rested with the facilities at Liverpool. The tides only allowed the ship to dock there every two months. (The lack of adequate docking arrangements was one of the reasons White Star had based the *Olympic* at Southampton in 1911.) After conferring with various officials, it was decided that the French port of Brest would be a more suitable eastern termination point for the liner. Brest was a deep water installation that was not affected by the tides to the extent Liverpool was. Another bonus of using Brest instead of a British port was that the soldiers' real destination was France anyway, further speeding up the process of getting the troops to the battlefront. The *Leviathan* could also be refueled with coal shipped from Liverpool at the same time she was offloading soldiers, greatly speeding up the preparations for the return to Hoboken.

The *Leviathan* left her homeport for Brest on 24 April 1918. She arrived at Brest on 2 May after a fairly uneventful and pleasant trip that was only marred by very thick fog as the troop transport approached land. Speed was reduced for a time and the escorts could barely be sighted in the mist. Finally, the harbour was located and the ship tied up to a large buoy. The *Leviathan* discharged her 8,909 troops and took on board over 4,600 tons of coal. Only three days after reaching Brest the liner departed for home, docking at Pier 4 on 12 May. The turnaround time for the *Leviathan* would drop to an average of only 26 days. The switch in ports had certainly increased the vessel's efficiency in delivering her precious cargo to the battlefields.

MENU
SUNDAY, APRIL 20, 1919

Breakfast
Oat Meal   Milk
Boiled Eggs
Fresh Fruit
Bread and Butter
Coffee

Dinner
Turkey
Tinned Asparagus   Mashed Potatoes
Pie and Cake
Bread and Butter
Coffee

Supper
Head Cheese
Creamed Potatoes
Bread and Butter
Coffee

Quantities Used to Provide the Above

	Lbs.		
Oat Meal	1150	Milk	480
Milk	1056	Sugar	400
Sugar	1500	Salt	40
Eggs (doz.)	3180	Cake	5740
Butter	660	Head Cheese	425
Apples	6470	Potatoes	800
Coffee	400	Coffee	200
Milk	480	Sugar	200
Salt	10	Salt	20
Turkey	15581	Bake Shop:	
Chicken	2021	Flour	7800
Asparagus	2856	Yeast	135
Mashed Potatoes	5850	Lard	130
Butter	675	Salt	100
Coffee	400	Sugar	200
		Cinnamon	4

Rations issued to 13,699.

A menu for the *Levi* while she was a troopship. (Author's collection)

Voyage number 4 would bring the former *Vaterland* face-to-face with the German U-boat threat. With her troop capacity boosted yet again, the liner left the US on 22 May 1918 with 10,577 troops aboard. Captain Henry Bryan was in command. The weather was clear and the sea quite calm for most of the journey. The excitement began when word was received on 29 May that the USS *Carlton* had been torpedoed and sunk directly in the area the *Leviathan* would steam through that evening. The course was altered and all possible precautions were taken to avoid the submarine. Nerves were frayed that night as the liner passed through the danger zone. The bright moon did not help matters since the light deprived the ship of her valuable cloak of darkness.

THE U.S.S. LEVIATHAN

Comparison of the Fifteen Leading Transports

(From *The Transport Ace*, Newspaper printed on board the "Leviathan")

The following comparison shows the number of round trips made, and the number of troops carried to Europe, by the fifteen leading transports up to the time the Armistice was signed, November 11, 1918.

Ship	No. of round trips	Largest No. in one trip	Total troops carried
Leviathan	10	10,860	119,215*
George Washington	9	5,529	46,159
President Grant	8	5,811	44,182
America	9	5,327	39,674
Agamemnon	10	4,917	35,026
Mount Vernon	9	4,763	33,549
Great Northern	10	3,058	27,590
Aeolus	8	3,551	24,327
President Lincoln	5	4,888	23,438
Northern Pacific	10	2,755	21,903
Martha Washington	8	3,055	21,900
Covington	6	4,133	21,754
Princess Matoika	6	3,865	21,163
Huron	8	2,917	20,771
Pocahontas	9	2,920	20,474

* The total of 119,215 for the *Leviathan* includes Naval Supernumeraries and crew carried on the first ten Eastbound trips. The present voyage makes the 14th round trip for this vessel.

The greatest number of persons carried by the *Leviathan* was on our sixteenth westbound trip when we had on board (including Naval Crew), a total of 14,300 persons.

The *Levi* had an impressive record in the First World War. (Author's collection)

THE U.S.S. LEVIATHAN

Daily Routine at Sea

A. M.
- 2:00 Relieve wheel and lookouts.
- 3:50 Call the watch section.
- 4:00 Relieve the watch. Muster the watch section and life boat's crew. Light smoking lamp. Call ship's cooks of the watch. Five minutes before sunrise station details at running lights. Turn off at sunrise. Relieve lookouts and station masthead lookouts.
- 5:00 Call idlers and section of the watch sleeping in. Coffee.
- 5:20 Pipe sweepers.
- 5:30 Turn to. Out smoking lamp. Execute morning orders.
- 5:00 Relieve the wheel and lookouts. Trice up clothes lines.
- 6:45 Hammock stowers haul back hammock cloths.
- 7:00 Up all hammocks.
- 7:15 Hammock stowers stop down hammock clothes. Mess Gear. Light smoking lamp.
- 7:30 Breakfast. Shift into the uniform of the day during the meal hour.
- 8:00 Relieve the watch; both sections on deck. Muster watch and life boat's crew.
- 8:15 Turn to. Out smoking lamp. Deck and gun bright work.
- 8:30 Sick call.
- 8:45 Knock off bright work. Sweep down. Stow away ditty boxes and wash deck gear. Take down towel lines. Clear up decks for quarters.
- 9:10 Officers' Call. Divisions fall in for quarters.
- 9:15 Quarters for muster and inspection. Physical drill and drills as prescribed.
- 10:00 Relieve the wheel and masthead.
- 11:30 Retreat from drill. Pipe down washed clothes, if dry. Sweep down.
- 11:45 Mess gear.

M.
- 12:00 Dinner.

P. M.
- 12:30 Relieve the watch.
- 1:00 Turn to. Pipe sweepers. Out smoking lamp.
- 1:45 Abandon ship drill call.
- 2:00 Relieve the wheel and masthead.
- 2:15 Retreat from drill. Pipe sweepers. Turn to.
- 3:30 Pipe down wash clothes, if up.
- 4:00 Relieve the watch. Muster watch and life boat's crew.
- 4:30 Sweep down. Knock off ship's work. Light smoking lamp. Five minutes before sunset station details at running lights. Turn on running lights with senior ship present. Station deck lookouts. Muster life boat's crew. Inspect life boats.
- 5:30 Clear up decks. Stow away ditty boxes.
- 5:45 Mess gear.
- 6:00 Supper. Relieve the wheel and lookouts.
- 6:30 Turn to. Sweep down. Wet down after raindeck.
- 7:00 Band concert for crew until 8:00.
- 7:30 Hammocks. No smoking below decks.
- 8:00 Call the watch. Relieve the wheel and lookouts. Relieve the watch. Muster watch and life boat's crew. Turn out all but standing lights and lights in officers' quarters and chief petty officers' mess room.
- 9:00 Out smoking lamp. Turn out lights in chief petty officers' mess room.
- 10:00 Relieve the wheel and lookout. Turn out lights in officers' quarters unless an extension has been granted.
- 11:50 Call the watch.
- Midnight. Relieve the watch. Muster the watch and life boat crew.

The daily schedule aboard USS *Leviathan*. (Author's collection)

A posed image of troops aboard *Leviathan*. (US Library of Congress)

A postcard view of the *Vaterland* laid up in New York during the First World War. (Author's collection)

USS *Leviathan* at NYC. (Author's collection)

The inevitable first encounter of the *Leviathan* with a U-boat came on 30 May. As the ship approached Brest and prepared to take aboard the pilot to guide the liner the rest of the way into port, a periscope was spotted off the port side at a distance of about 4,500ft. The engine room telegraphs were rung full speed ahead and the guns were trained on the submarine. For the next hour a submarine appeared twice more and a total of nineteen shots were fired by the *Leviathan* at her foe. A French fishing boat was nearly caught in the vessel's gunfire, but fortunately was not hit. It is possible that the ship actually saw three different submarines that had been stationed in predetermined positions to increase the chances of catching the liner before she reached Brest. Luckily for the ship and crew, however, the attempt was unsuccessful and the *Leviathan* tied up at her normal buoy later in the afternoon.

But the adventure was not over for the crew of the *Leviathan*. After departing Brest on 1 June she once again had to deal with enemy U-boats. The Germans desperately wanted to sink the valuable transport, once the pride of their merchant marine. The Kaiser offered a $10,000 reward for her destruction. The wake of a periscope was spotted around 7.15pm. The ship surged ahead at top speed and the gun crews opened fire. Two destroyers dropped depth charges near the submarine's position, but the U-boat was not seen again. The *Leviathan* arrived back at Hoboken on 8 June. It had been a nerve-wracking voyage.

The *Leviathan* quickly settled into her routine as a troop carrier. She frequently transported over 10,000 troops to France. Voyage number 9 was sadly notable because of an outbreak of influenza on board. The trip began on 29 September 1918 and ended on 7 October with her arrival at Brest. A total of 96 people had died from the disease. It was a crossing most on board wanted to forget.

On 3 November the *Leviathan* tied up at Liverpool on her tenth voyage as a troop ship. (Liverpool was substituted for Brest since the ship was in need of dry-docking.) The last few hours of the trip had been eventful when fog forced a delay in docking and the ship ran aground and was stranded for seven hours. The liner was once again placed in the Gladstone dry dock. The crew exploded into celebration on 11 November when it was announced that Germany had surrendered. The war was over, but this did not mean the *Leviathan* was no longer needed by the military. Over 119,000 troops had been carried by the *Leviathan* to Europe on ten round trips. (Her closest US competitor, the ex-NDL liner *George Washington*, had moved about 46,000 on nine voyages.) She had taken one out of every twenty American soldiers to the fields of battle and now she had to bring them back.

After a month of work, the *Leviathan* left Liverpool on 4 December 1918 with wounded soldiers aboard. The next day she arrived at her customary buoy at Brest and began to refuel and embark troops for the journey home. The liner departed Brest on 8 December and reached New York on 15 December. To say the ship was given a warm welcome was an understatement. Thousands gathered to watch some of the first troops returning home since the end of the war. Small boats crowded the harbour and their bells and whistles echoed across the water. Many of the soldiers were quite moved by the incredible reception. It had been exactly one year since the *Leviathan* had first left Hoboken with troops aboard. With the uncertainty of war now gone, however, this was a much happier occasion.

Christmas 1918 was to be a memorable one for over 1,200 orphaned children. They were treated to a day on the big ship. A huge dinner was made for them and Santa Claus made a grand entrance by climbing down a funnel! He, of course, provided a present for each child. The children were also given a tour of the largest vessel in the world. The American Red Cross also had gifts for the crew. Each bag had cigarettes, pipes, tobacco and candy. It was an enjoyable time for all.

As with any ship, the *Leviathan* had been given several nicknames by her wartime passengers. Some called her the 'Levi-Nathan', while others referred to her as simply the '*Levi*.' She had earned an enviable reputation as a troop carrier and quickly became a household name across the country. An ex-German vessel had become one of the most famous American liners in the world.

With the conflict over it was decided to increase the troop capacity of the *Leviathan* to its maximum. Provisions were made for the carrying of over 14,000 people. This was unheard of for the time and would require careful planning. The troops would have to be assigned to certain sections of the ship since too many on one side could cause a considerable, even dangerous, list. On board supplies would have to be increased substantially to house so many soldiers. But with the war over, the risk was considered minimal in transporting such a huge number at one time in a single ship. It was seen as the most efficient use of available resources. It would also give the *Leviathan* yet another place in the history books.

The start of 1919 saw the *Leviathan* plunging into her new duties as a repatriation vessel. She departed New York for Brest on Voyage 11 on 24 January. She returned on 11 February with 11,899 aboard. Voyage 13, completed on 2 April, delivered 14,416 people to Hoboken. This was a world record for the number of people aboard a ship at one time. This benchmark would not be broken until the *Queen Mary* embarked 16,683 in the Second World War.

In May, the *Leviathan* was reunited with her sistership *Imperator*. She had sat out the war in Germany and was taken over by the Allies and put under the control of the US Now christened USS *Imperator*, she was quickly fitted out as a troop transport to aide in bringing American soldiers home. A friendly rivalry developed when the two liners raced each other to New York. Despite departing nine hours after the *Imperator* on 13 May, the *Leviathan* caught up with and passed her sister on the 17th. The *Imperator* managed to stay within visual range of the *Levi* for the rest of the trip, however. Both ships tied up at Hoboken on 23 May.

The troop-carrying days of the *Leviathan* came to an end in September 1919. She completed Voyage 19 early in the month and was discharged from government service. Over the course of her military career, the *Levi* had transported over 192,000 people across the Atlantic. It had been a huge exercise in organisation from the start to operate such a massive liner safely and effectively. It was a very impressive performance for the US Navy, especially considering that they did not have any vessels that even approached *Leviathan* in size at the start of the war. Many said it could not be done, but they were proven wrong. The *Leviathan* had shown the world the vital role of ocean liners in wartime. These lessons were to prove invaluable in the even more destructive conflict that was only two decades away.

This extraordinary image from 1919 shows the sisterships *Imperator* and *Leviathan* reunited at Hoboken. The *Imperator* had been seized by US forces at the war's close and was pressed into troop-carrying duty. The changes made to the design of the bridge front of the *Imperator* and ex-*Vaterland* can be seen here. The huge searchlight on the *Leviathan*'s mast is also visible. (US Naval Historical Archives)

The *Levi* arrives at the Newport News Shipyards for her long-awaited conversion into a passenger liner for USL. (Author's collection)

four

What to do with a Leviathan?

With her trooping duties behind her, the *Leviathan* was once again idle at Hoboken. Her future was very much in doubt. Many said that such a large ship could never earn her keep in passenger service and that she should be used in some kind of static role – perhaps to shelter the homeless. Others hoped that she would be reconditioned and run with the *Imperator* under the US flag. This would have given America a formidable presence on the North Atlantic. But it was not to be. The *Imperator* was handed over to Cunard as a replacement for the *Lusitania* on 19 September 1919. She would later be renamed *Berengaria* and became the flagship of the post-war Cunard fleet. The final sister, the incomplete *Bismarck*, would eventually be finished in 1922 and join the White Star fleet as the *Majestic*. She took the place of the *Britannic*, which had been sunk by a mine in November 1916. With a small skeleton crew on board to provide minimal maintenance and security, the *Leviathan* awaited her next call to duty.

Unfortunately that call would be a long time coming. Politics would take the centre stage and deprive the *Levi* of a proper place in the Atlantic express service. It would be years before she would journey into the open sea once more. With the average lifespan of an ocean liner before the Second World War being about 25 years, any time laid up was time lost for the *Leviathan*. But there was hope.

The US Navy transferred the *Levi* and several other vessels to the US Shipping Board in late 1919. Shortly thereafter, the Shipping Board assigned the *Leviathan* to IMM. Plans were made to refurbish the *Levi* and operate her under the banner of the American Line. This once proud company had fallen behind in the transatlantic race and was dying a slow death. At the turn of the century, the American Line had four excellent liners: the *St Louis*, *St Paul*, *New York* and *Philadelphia*. Although not the largest or fastest ships on the ocean, these vessels were quite elegant and offered modern accommodation. Plans were even made to build a 1,000ft superliner, but this unfortunately never came to pass.

IMM was an excellent choice to manage the *Leviathan*. They had considerable experience and were international in scope, even though American owned. IMMCO had the ability to solve a problem for both the American Line and White Star. A very important part of the transatlantic express run was the capability of offering a balanced service with three comparable liners providing a weekly departure from both sides of the Atlantic. Although the American Line could offer nothing of the *Leviathan*'s size and quality, White Star could. In 1920, the *Olympic* triumphantly returned to passenger service after an exemplary war record and quickly captured a large share of the trade. But she was essentially a loner without proper running mates. The *Majestic* would fill some of the gap in 1922, but a third ship was still needed. The *Levi* would have fit in perfectly. White Star would have had a superb express service to compete with Cunard's *Berengaria*, *Aquitania* and *Mauretania*. But circumstances would force the *Levi* to run by herself and White Star would have to make do with the ex-NDL liner *Columbus* (renamed *Homeric*). Although an excellent vessel, her cruising speed of 18 knots did not make her an ideal partner for *Olympic* and *Majestic*. Both companies would be cheated of an almost perfectly matched set of ships by an odd

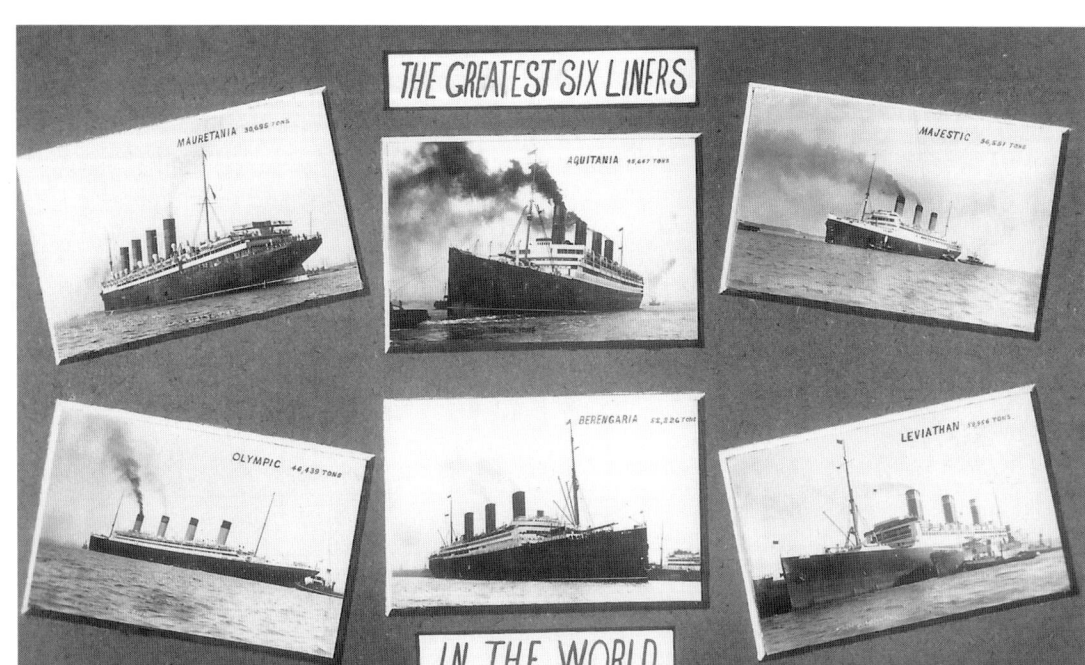

A postcard showing the 'Greatest Six Liners in the World': *Leviathan*, *Majestic*, *Berengaria*, *Olympic*, *Aquitania* & *Mauretania*. (Author's collection)

An excellent post-war photograph of the *'Levi-Nathan'* in New York. Her lines are shown to good form in this view. (Author's collection)

The 'Aztec Suite'. (Author's collection)

Perhaps the finest public room afloat at the time-the *Levi*'s Social Hall. (Author's collection)

Basic information about the American flagship. (Author's collection)

A secluded section of the smoking room. (Author's collection)

A suite bedroom. (Author's collection)

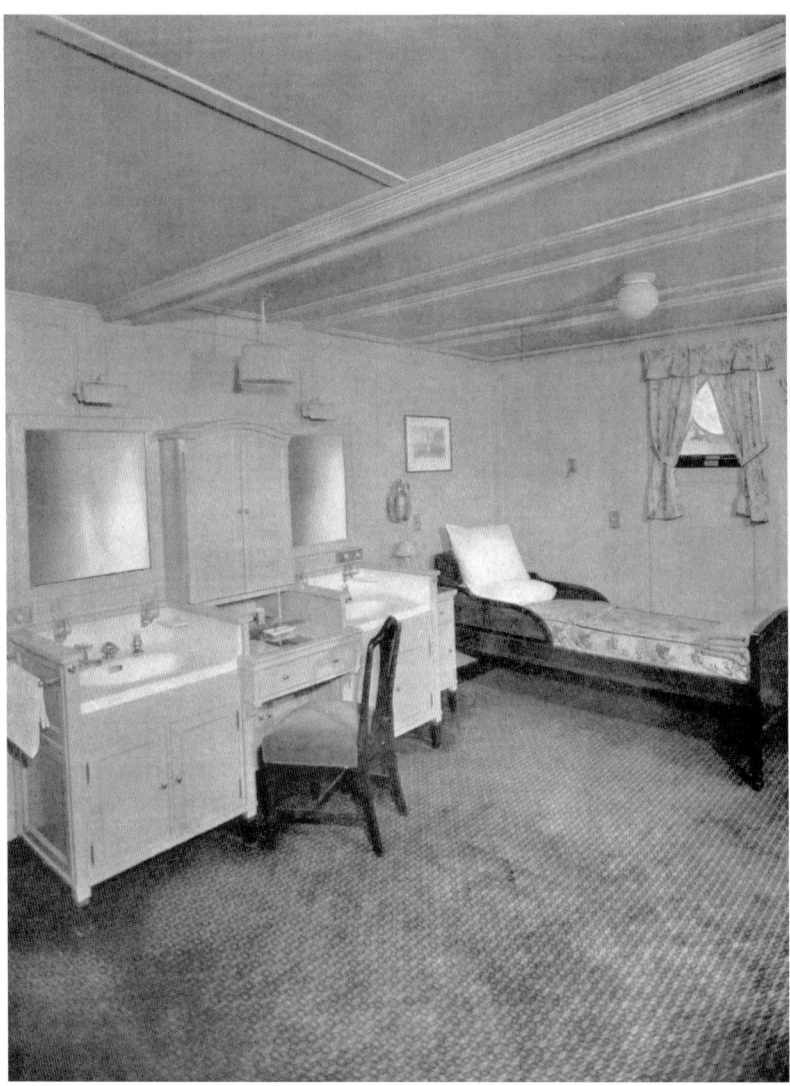

An 'Outside Room' of a first class suite. (Author's collection)

What to do with a Leviathan? 45

A bathroom can be seen in this image of a first class suite. (Author's collection)

The Promenade Deck. (Author's collection)

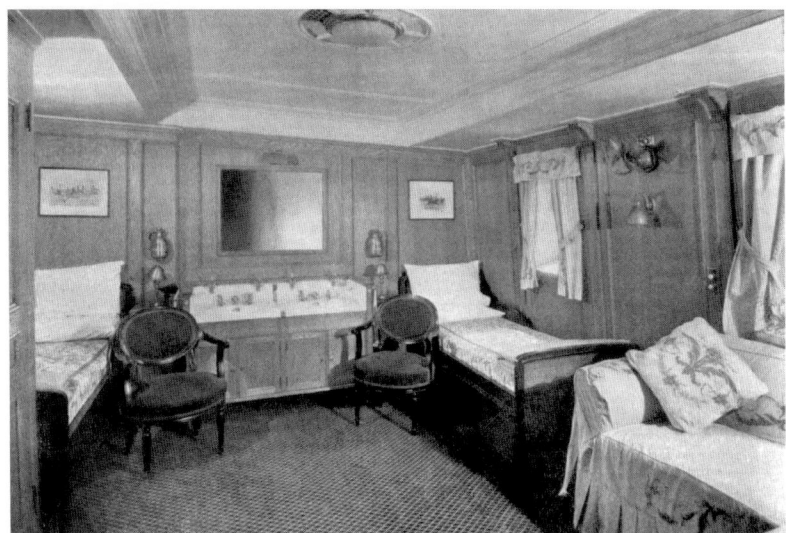

An 'outside room' for a first class suite. (Author's collection)

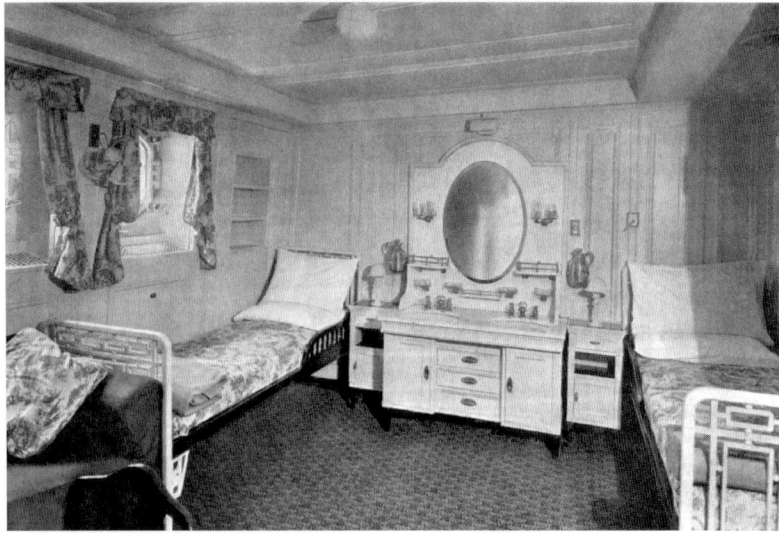

Another 'outside room' for a first class suite. (Author's collection)

political situation that ended any chance of IMM acquiring the *Levi* in the 1920s.

If one man was responsible for the events that denied the *Leviathan* to IMM, it was William Randolph Hearst. Born in San Francisco in 1863, Hearst went on to develop the concept of the modern newspaper we know today. He eventually owned nearly thirty newspaper companies in the US. His papers were accused of inventing interviews, stretching the facts and following a philosophy we would call today tabloid journalism. Hearst's newspapers quickly condemned the plan to sell the *Leviathan* and other ex-German liners to IMM. The main charge was that IMM could transfer the *Levi* and the other ships to the British flag. The British Navy could then requisition the vessels for war service at any time. The papers also argued that the sale price was too low and was a virtual giveaway to a company that controlled British shipping lines. The whole 'debate' quickly deteriorated into a twisted mess of questionable facts and half truths. IMMCO President P.A.S. Franklin did not help matters when he told reporters that he did not know if the *Levi* would operate under the American flag or not. Eventually, Hearst himself filed a lawsuit and an injunction for the sale was granted. In early 1922 IMM backed down and withdrew their bid. The American Line closed its doors soon after.

With IMM out of the picture, the question once again was raised about finding suitable running mates for the *Leviathan*. The solution seemed to be the ex-NDL 4-stackers *Agamemnon* and *Mt. Vernon*. Formerly the *Kaiser Wilhelm II* and *Kronprinzessin Cecilie* respectively, these two liners would have made acceptable partners for the *Levi*. Although considerably smaller than the *Leviathan*, they could cruise at close to 23 knots, creating a balanced express service at least in terms of speed. Over the years, various plans would be drawn up but in the end, sadly, the ships would never see service again. They would be laid up in Chesapeake Bay for many years and would eventually be sold for breaking up in 1940 due to their poor condition. Two other former German vessels, however, were refitted and put into passenger service under the stars and stripes – the *Amerika* (re-named *America*) and *George Washington*. Both ships were roughly 24,000 tons and cruised at around 18 knots. Although well appointed and comfortable ships, they were not suitable partners for the *Leviathan* since they had been built as intermediate type liners. The *Agamemnon* and *Mt Vernon* would

Another view of the Social Hall. (Author's collection)

A rare view of the tea room. (Author's collection)

The fireplace in the first class smoking room. (Author's collection)

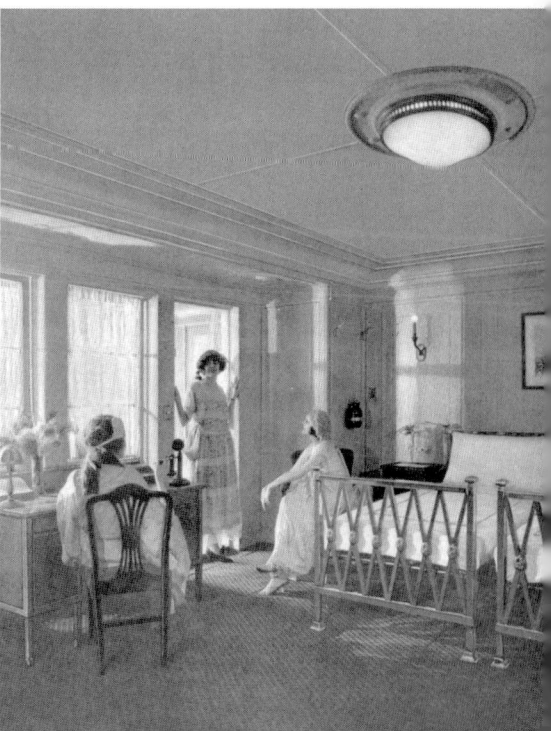

A corner of the smoking room. This room was still considered a male preserve in the 1920s. (Author's collection)

A luxurious first class stateroom. (Author's collection)

The accommodations in first class truly lived up to the expectations of the typical well-to-do passenger. (Author's collection)

The more expensive staterooms in first class included a 'breakfast room'. (Author's collection)

A sitting room in first class. (Author's collection)

This image gives the viewer a warm and cozy feeling – precisely what USL wanted. (Author's collection)

The second class social hall. (Author's collection)

The second class social lobby. (Author's collection)

What to do with a Leviathan? 49

Above Looking forward from the stern. (Author's collection)

Above The *Levi* begins her triumphant sea trials in 1923. (Author's collection)

Left Information for *Leviathan* passengers. (Author's collection)

Left An ad for the Sperry Gyro-Compass features Captain Hartley. (Author's collection)

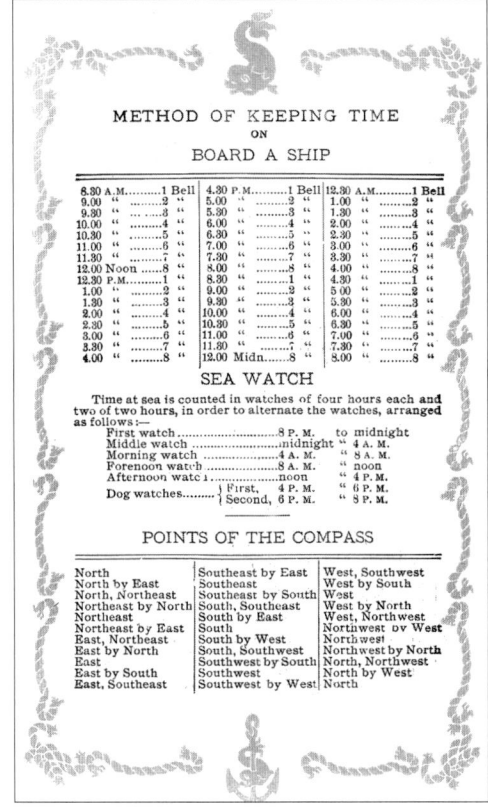

Left This USL document explains how the watches were kept on the ship. (Author's collection)

Below Workers leave the *Levi* during her massive refurbishment at Newport News. (Author's collection)

Below This rare copy of the log of the Leviathan's trails in 1923 shows the impressive speeds she attained, albeit with the help of the current. (Author's collection)

What to do with a Leviathan? 51

Right The Gyro Compass was a very sophisticated instrument for its day. (Author's collection)

Below This panel indicated the presence of any fires on board the liner. This was state-of-the-art for the time. (Author's collection)

Right One of the dynamos that provided electric power for the on-board systems. (Author's collection)

Below The first class galley had to prepare countless meals per day. (Author's collection)

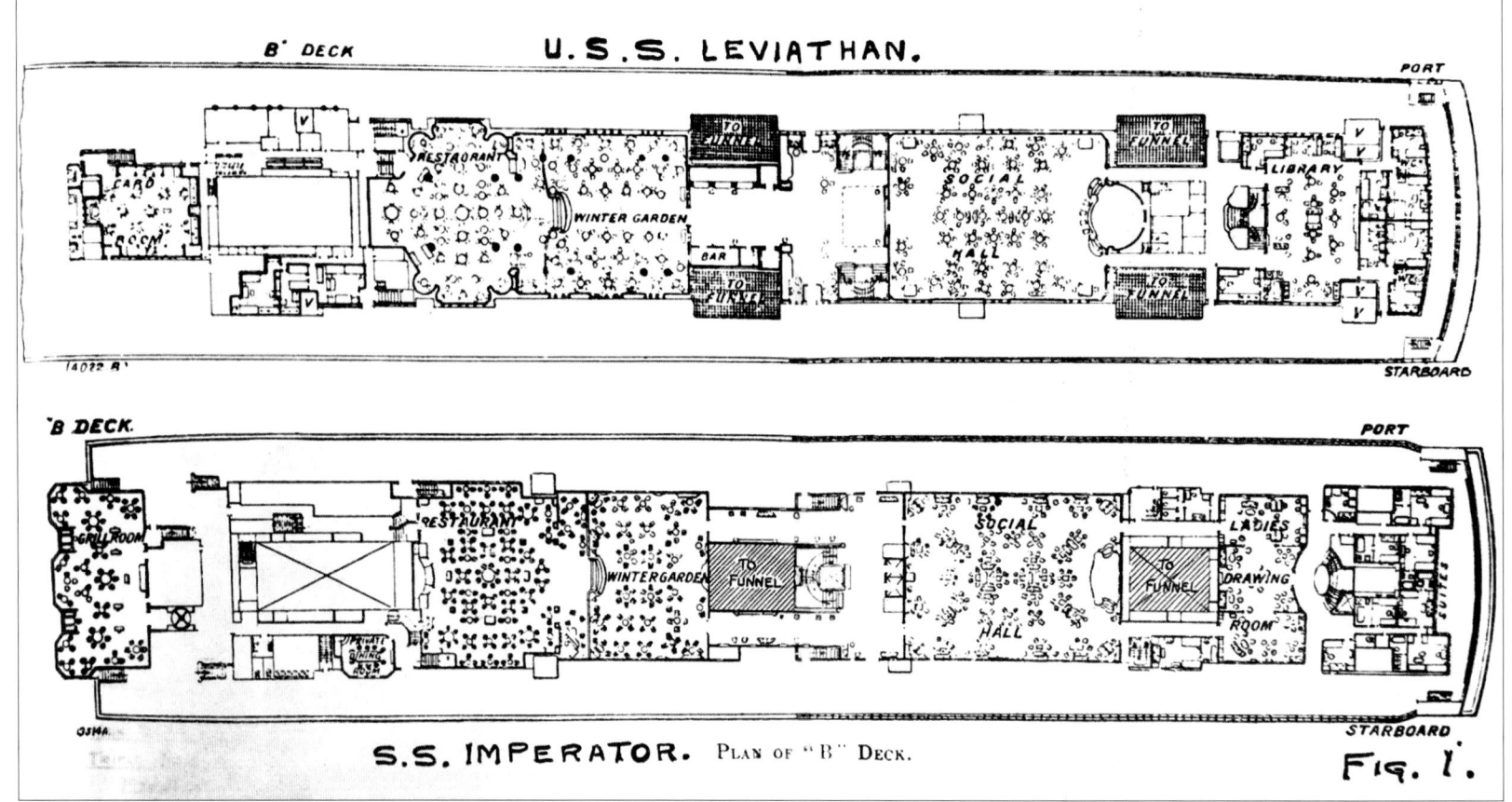

This deck plan shows how the split uptakes of the *Vaterland/Leviathan* allowed for uninterrupted space for public rooms through the centerline of B-Deck. The *Imperator/Berengaria* used standard uptakes. (Author's collection)

have been better choices for refurbishment. This was yet another of the misfortunes the *Leviathan* would endure during her time under the American flag.

Another blow came in the defeat of a subsidy bill in Congress. The proposed law would have provided financial assistance to enable US commercial vessels to better compete against foreign rivals that had lower operating costs. The bill would have provided the *Leviathan* with a payment of about $1,000,000 annually from the government. The loss of the subsidy further hampered the chances of the *Levi* being a financial success in her early years.

A further setback for the *Levi*, and liners in general, was the end of unrestricted immigration to the US after the war. While about a million people had immigrated to America every year before the First World War, new government quotas reduced this dramatically by 1923. The Emergency Immigration Act of 1921 set the maximum number of immigrants allowed into the US at 357,000 per year (about 800,000 had entered the country in 1920). Ships such as the *Leviathan* had been designed to carry large amounts of steerage class passengers and the loss of this traffic was a major problem for the transatlantic liner business. A partial solution was to create a new class designation,

What to do with a Leviathan? 53

Above The starboard portion of A-Deck. (Rich Turnwald collection)

Right SS Leviathan: The flagship of the American Merchant Marine in the twenties and thirties. (Rich Turnwald collection)

A good broadside view of the handsome Leviathan. (Rich Turnwald collection)

Above The *Levi* at sea in a postcard view. (Author's collection)

Left An aerial view of the *Levi* at NYC. (Steamship Historical Society of America)

tourist third. Former third class sections of liners were revamped and offered to eager, but budget minded, middle class travellers. The plan worked to some extent, but the enormous passenger lists of the big liners was seldom repeated in the post-war era.

While the political wrangling raged on, plans to return the *Levi* to service continued, albeit at a slower pace than expected. William Francis Gibbs entered the picture at this point. Gibbs was born in 1886. He and his younger brother, Frederic, developed a passion for ocean vessels at a young age. His father, however, pushed him to become a lawyer and he graduated with a law degree in 1913. But his real passion lay with passenger ships. In 1916 Gibbs Brothers was founded by William and Frederic. The new company had won a contract from IMMCO to design two 1,000ft-long liners that would cruise at close to 30 knots and create the first two-ship Atlantic express service in history; they were tentatively named *Boston* and *Baltimore*. The fact that William had accomplished this without any formal engineering training was remarkable. Unfortunately, the coming of the Great War put the planned ships on the back burner and Gibbs Brothers was forced to concentrate their energy on the war effort. However, in only a few short years Gibbs would be called upon to embark on one of the most difficult, and rewarding, jobs of his life.

When the *Leviathan* was assigned to IMMCO in 1919 it was no surprise that William Francis Gibbs was given the task of refitting her for commercial service once again. The ship would keep his firm occupied for several years. Gibbs relished the chance to renovate the vessel and prove his talents. He immediately ran into a problem that seemed like a stone wall – there were no detailed schematics for the liner. All had been destroyed or hidden by the *Vaterland*'s crew before the ship was seized by the US government. When asked to provide the plans, Blohm & Voss coolly replied that they would do so, for $1,000,000. Gibbs would not give up so easily, though. With about sixty draftsmen at his side, he crawled around the *Leviathan* for the next year and a half and drew up his own plans for the great ship. The Herculean effort cost about $250,000. With the plan in hand, Gibbs then made arrangements for the extensive overhaul that would transform a tired troopship into a luxurious ocean liner. But, once again, politics would derail his ambitions to have the *Leviathan* sailing again in 1921 or 1922.

With IMM gone it seemed that no US shipping firm had the resources or experience to run the *Levi* on the highly competitive Atlantic. There seemed to be only one choice: create a new company. In 1923 United States Lines (USL) was formed as a government-owned

The attempts to 'Americanise' the original German scrollwork on the *Leviathan*'s stern can be seen in this photograph. (Author's collection)

business. A white flag with USL in the middle was adopted as the symbol of the fledgling line. It was hoped that eventually US Lines would be sold to commercial interests since many felt government operation was inefficient and went against the American tradition of a privately run free market system. But the most important thing was that the *Leviathan* had an operator. Now a substantial sum of money was needed to return her to service.

Once again, the government came to the rescue. The US Congress passed a bill that provided over $8,000,000 to the *Leviathan* project. On 15 February 1922 Newport News Shipyards of Norfolk, Virginia received the contract for the reconditioning of the *Levi*. The years of political squabbling were over. The *Leviathan* was coming back; it was only a matter of time.

The SS *Leviathan*, pride of the American Merchant Marine. (Author's collection)

The *Leviathan* in a contemporary postcard. (Author's collection)

58 SS Leviathan

The *Levi* at or near the Naval Drydock in Boston, Massachusetts, on various dates. (Author's collection)

What to do with a Leviathan? 59

The *Levi* at or near the Naval Drydock in Boston, Massachusetts, on various dates. (Author's collection)

Opposite, left *Levi* at or near the Naval Drydock in Boston, Massachusetts, on various dates. (Author's collection)

Right and opposite, right The *Levi* at or near the Naval Drydock in Boston, Massachusetts, on various dates. (Author's collection)

62 SS Leviathan

Levi at or near the Naval Drydock in Boston, Massachusetts, on various dates. (Author's collection)

APRIL 5, 1930

five

World's Greatest Ship

The *Leviathan* quickly moved out of her Hoboken dock on 9 April 1922. She was bound for the Newport News shipyards and a new lease on life. Shortly after departure a thick fog settled in and speed had to be reduced. The frequently temperamental steering gear was slow to respond to commands and failed at one point. This forced the ship to manoeuvre on her propellers only – not the best way to handle such an enormous vessel. She arrived at Pier 1 at Newport News the next day and was secured by 9.09a.m. Work to recondition her began almost immediately. There was little time to waste since she was expected to be ready for service in mid-1923. The long delay meant that the third *Imperator* Class liner, the *Bismarck*, was completed and handed over to White Star at about the time the *Levi* tied up at the shipyards. With the name *Majestic* painted on her bows, she proudly steamed into New York City on 17 May as the largest liner in the world. With the *Berengaria* (ex-*Imperator*) also in service for Cunard, the competition was heating up.

For a brief time the *Leviathan* was renamed the *President Harding*, but the president himself intervened and requested that she be returned to her old name. He argued that the liner should keep the name she had become known for during her sterling war service. There was little disagreement on this point.

The most important, and expensive, modification made to the *Levi* during the overhaul was the conversion of her boilers to burn oil instead of coal. This was projected to cost nearly $6,000,000, about 73 per cent of the refurbishment budget. Long term, however, it was a logical choice. The Peabody Engineering oil burning installation improved engine efficiency and reduced labor costs since the 400 stockers, or black gang, would no longer be required. Each boiler was fitted with five oil burners. One person could supervise the operation of at least two boilers. The disposal of ashes also became a thing of the past. Oil also provided more energy when compared to coal: six tons of oil could do the same work as ten tons of coal. The ship could be refuelled much more quickly in port, allowing quicker turnarounds and more voyages per year. The problem of coal dust seeping into the passenger accommodation would also be eliminated, reducing cleaning expenses. The *Levi* was fitted with a capacity for 9,563 tons of oil stored in 46 tanks in the inner skin and double bottom. Steam pressure was increased to 248lb psi compared to 235 when built as a coal burner. Fuel consumption would be around 900 tons daily.

The engines of the ship were also thoroughly reconditioned and the steering gear was repaired. With the engines overhauled and the new oil fuel system, it was anticipated that the ship would be faster than ever. The liner was also rewired with the superior 'two-way' electrical system that was much safer than the original wiring. The *Levi* would never suffer the number of fires that would plague her sisters.

The interiors were carefully restored to their pre-war glory. Despite USL statements to the contrary, few changes were made to her passenger spaces since the original German interiors were considered more than adequate. It was a big job, however, since portions of the Hapag fittings had been carelessly ripped out and destroyed during the troop ship conversion. Expert woodworkers were necessary in order to duplicate the ornate carving in the panelling. Her new passenger

Above A virtual fleet of tugs assist the *Leviathan* in her first year of service with USL. (Author's collection)

Above The elegant interiors of one of the *Levi*'s competitors, the *Aquitania*, are highlighted in this period postcard. (Author's collection)

Below Captain Hartley and the officers of the *Leviathan* in 1923. (Author's collection)

Left An advertisement for the fleet of United States Lines in the 1920s. (Author's collection)

A powered lifeboat of the *Levi*. (Author's collection)

The massive steering gear of the *Levi*. (Author's collection)

One of the 'Silent Salts' figures in the first class smoking room. (Author's collection)

capacity was listed as 976 first class; 542 second class; 944 third class; and 936 steerage cass. The total passenger load was 3,398 in all classes. With a crew of 1,115, the *Levi* could carry 4,513 people on one trip, 630 less than her pre-war total.

Gibbs Brothers was also concerned about safety and modifications were made to reduce the probability of a major disaster sending the *Levi* to the bottom of the ocean. The original ventilation system for the boiler rooms was ripped out and replaced by an arrangement considered to be more watertight. All of the portholes below F-deck were permanently sealed to reduce the risk of water flowing into them in the event the ship took on a severe list after being damaged in a collision. Indeed, a single open porthole could allow four tons of water to enter the ship every minute. The White Star Liner *Britannic*, sistership to *Olympic* and *Titanic*, had been sunk during the war when she struck a mine and open portholes allowed otherwise undamaged watertight compartments to flood. This meant that there was not an open porthole within 20ft of the waterline in normal conditions. Some of the watertight bulkheads were strengthened and raised in height. A watertight deck was also added above the engine room. Of the original 33 watertight doors installed during construction, only fifteen remained after the rebuild. Since these doors can malfunction (faulty watertight doors contributed to *Britannic*'s loss) and not close properly, Gibbs thought it prudent to eliminate as many of them as possible. Although officially designated a three compartment ship, meaning she could stay afloat with three compartments flooded, Gibbs stated that she could actually survive up to five breached compartments in certain situations. The original longitudinal watertight bulkheads, which ran along the length of the boiler and engine rooms, also provided an extra margin by confining the flooding to the inner skin. This could also cause a problem, however, since a ship could take on a severe list if too many longitudinal sections were opened on one side of the vessel. To help with this, the pumping equipment was improved substantially. The bilge pumps could drain nearly 1,800 tons per hour from the ship if necessary.

The lifeboat accommodations were also modified. Seventy-two lifeboats were provided in all. This was more than enough to evacuate every person on board. Twenty-two of the boats would be made of metal and had a capacity of fifty people each. Special note was made of a 'life towboat' that had a 100hp diesel engine and could tow a large number of standard lifeboats behind it. The boat was described as the only one of its kind and was 'non-capsizable.'

As the refit neared completion, William Francis Gibbs became determined to extract the maximum amount of favorable publicity for

The ship's bell. (Author's collection)

The *Leviathan* even had her own bank. (Author's collection)

the *Leviathan*. He did so by not only setting out to declare the *Levi* the largest ship in the world, but also the fastest. How he accomplished this feat was an indication of his deep understanding of how regulations and figures could be manipulated to tell a story that was not a direct lie, but at the very minimum a stretch of the facts.

Gross Registered Tonnage (GRT), is the primary method of measuring the size of passenger ships. One hundred cu. ft of enclosed space equals one ton. However, there were different rules adopted by nations that made the whole task of judging a vessel's size confusing and open to interpretation. The British rules essentially measured the entire vessel, but American regulations only accounted for the hull and two superstructure decks in the tonnage calculations. It was also debatable as to what defined 'enclosed' space. This left room for manipulation of a liner's tonnage. Gibbs decided to take full advantage of this. He used the British system and every conceivable part of the *Leviathan* that could be defined as enclosed, to raise her tonnage from 54,282 tons to 59,957 tons. The *Levi* was now the biggest ship in the world. The *Majestic* was 56,551 tons by comparison. Both liners would be advertised as the largest in the world for quite some time, a most unusual situation. Although White Star could have probably re-classified *Majestic* as being about 61,206 tons, in the end they chose to do nothing. Raising a vessel's tonnage by such a huge margin was unprecedented for the time without adding additional decks. A more reasonable example was White Star's *Olympic*. When she entered service in 1911, her tonnage was 45,324 whilst her sister *Titanic* came in at 46,329 tons the next year. After a post-*Titanic* disaster refit, *Olympic* was re-measured to 46,359 tons. Her final GRT was 46,439 tons in 1920. This only amounted to a change of 1,115 tons for *Olympic* during her career, while the *Levi* jumped 5,675 tons virtually overnight.

Another way to grab headlines was to arrange for the *Levi*'s trial run to take place in as favorable conditions as possible. It was announced that she would steam to Cuba on her sea trials. This would allow her to conduct speed tests in waters known for strong currents. The Gulf Stream could add up to four knots to the liner's speed. With some fine weather tossed in, the *Leviathan* had a good chance of making an impressive dash for a brief period.

It was announced in March 1923 that Captain Herbert Hartley had been named commander of the *Leviathan*. Born in Oswego Falls in New York in 1875, he went to sea while relatively young and was

INTERESTING FACTS AT SEA

TIME ON SHIPBOARD – Between New York and London there is a difference in time of five hours, and as the sun rises in the East, as we say, when the ship is going eastward she meets sunlight earlier each day and thus gains time. Exactly how much, is computed each day at noon, and the ship's clocks are immediately set at the correct time for that longitude. On a vessel which makes the crossing in five days the clocks will be set ahead each day approximately an hour; on slower ships, of course, less. Going westward the clock is set back daily in similar fashion.

On the voyage from Europe, owing to the alteration in time as the ship proceeds Westward, it is necessary to put the clock back every 24 hours. The alteration in time is made at about midnight, and the clock is usually put back 45 minutes on each occasion, the exact amount of time depending upon the distance the ship is estimated to make by noon the next day. During the first 24 hours, however, owing to the change from Mean Time to Apparent Time, the alteration is likely to be considerably more than 45 minutes, especially while Summer Time is in use.

Due to the fact that an ocean liner passes through several time zones on her journey, the keeping of time can be complex to the casual observer. How this is accomplished is explained here. (Author's collection)

A period postcard depicts the similar interiors of the *Levi*'s competitor and sistership, Cunard's *Berengaria*. (Author's collection)

Chief Officer of the *St Louis* during the war. Hartley had recently remarried and was planning to retire from the sea and move to Alabama with his new wife. All that changed however; when US Lines offered him the top post on the flagship of the American Merchant Marine. Who could turn down such a prestigious command?

As May 1923 approached, the excitement was building for the long-sought return of the *Leviathan* to the Atlantic. The drab troopship had been transformed once again into a luxury liner by the workers at Newport News. The grey hull was painted a shiny black, while the funnels glistened in their red, white and blue livery. Aside from the name on the bow and stern, and the changes in the lifeboat placements, the ship looked very much like her former German self. Hapag had built an exceptional vessel and massive improvements were not considered necessary. Although Americanised, the *Levi* would always carry reminders of her heritage; the most obvious being the ship's bell, which carried its original *Vaterland* engraving to the end of the ship's days.

As the *Leviathan* prepared to reclaim her spot on the Atlantic service, Prohibition reared its head. This amendment to the US Constitution in 1919 declared the sale of alcohol in the nation to be illegal. A court battle later ensued that involved whether or not American flagged vessels could carry liquor on board. The Supreme Court ruled that foreign liners could sell alcohol when outside the twelve-mile limit from the shore. They would, however, have to purchase their alcohol supplies in other countries. It was also deemed permissible for ships flying the stars and stripes to sell spirits outside the limit. Yet they could not dock in American ports with a level of alcohol above the amount allowed for medicinal purposes. Not surprisingly, a considerable bootleg business evolved on eastbound crossings when the supply was lower. Westbound trips were another matter since alcohol could be purchased easily overseas. Nonetheless, US vessels had to dump excess liquor overboard before entering national waters. (Although Captain Hartley claimed years later in his biography that he kept the Levi 'dry as a bone.') The whole affair was a complicated mess that went through several changes before the repeal of Prohibition in 1933. It did, most definitely, add an additional handicap to the economical operation of the *Levi* (although not as much as some people believe) that she did not need in such a fiercely competitive environment.

Before the trial run to Cuba, a dry docking was necessary to clean the hull. The big ship left Newport News on 16 May 1923 and headed

68   SS Leviathan

The *Levi* makes an impressive sight as she steams passed the Statue of Liberty. (Steamship Historical Society of America)

Promenading on the *Leviathan*. (Steamship Historical Society of America)

Below, left and right The *Levi* at or near the Naval Drydock in Boston, Massachusetts on various dates. (Author's collection)

The *Leviathan* passes her sistership Majestic. (Bill Miller collection)

In this overhead image, the *Leviathan*'s sistership *Majestic* makes an impressive sight at New York. (Author's collection)

north. She arrived at the Navy dry dock in Boston two days later. It took fifteen tugs to move her giant bulk into the dock. Several hours later, and after the draining of over 230,000 tons of water, the *Levi* was high and dry in the naval facility. Over the next month, a number of important tasks were completed. The rudder and screws were detached and inspected, bilge keels were added, rivets were examined, the hull carefully checked and cleared of barnacles and numerous other chores carried out in order to have the liner ready on schedule.

As planned the *Levi* was floated out of dry dock on 18 June. She took on board dignitaries and other guests and slowly made her way out of Boston Harbor the next day. Although some people in political circles had criticised the need for a trail run of a nine-year-old liner, USL responded that it was necessary since the ship had been given an extensive overhaul and it would give the crew valuable operating experience.

The *Leviathan*'s trials were a huge success. The ship performed magnificently, beyond the expectations of many experienced nautical observers. The voyage was headline news across the country. A world speed record – exactly what Gibbs had hoped for – was claimed when the liner averaged 27.94 knots from Jupiter Light (Florida) to Cape Henry in one day. She covered a total of 687 miles during that time. The *Levi* had also held 28 knots for 6 hours. It was now claimed that the United States had not only the largest vessel in the world, but also the fastest. The Cunard speed queen *Mauretania* had managed 27.04 knots on a similar run in 1911 and still held the Blue Riband. However, it is highly unlikely that the *Leviathan* could have beaten the *Mauretania* on an entire transatlantic crossing. Unlike the *Leviathan*, the *Mauretania* had been designed with the speed record in mind. She was lighter and had more horsepower per ton of displacement. Nonetheless, the trials had demonstrated that the *Levi* was one of the world's premier ocean going vessels and would prove to be a worthy competitor in the transatlantic passenger trade.

The *Leviathan* steamed triumphantly into New York harbour on 24 June and tied up at the freshly dredged Pier 86. Thousands of people were on hand to greet her. The United States had entered the 'Big Leagues' in the Atlantic passenger business. USL called their re-fitted superliner the 'World's Greatest Ship'. Now it was time to see if the *Leviathan* would live up to those expectations.

six

1923 – Back on the Atlantic

The *Leviathan* began her third 'maiden voyage' on 4 July 1923. It was a foggy and rainy day, but enthusiasm was high among New Yorkers. It may have seemed that most of the city showed up to see the ship off. The area around Pier 86 was packed with about 10,000 people. Visitors flocked aboard the liner in massive numbers (for some reason, USL issued over 10,000 guest passes). After about half of that number was on board, officials had had enough and ordered the *Levi* closed to visitors.

With three blasts from her whistles, the *Leviathan* gently slipped out of the south side of the pier. Her propellers churned the water and tugs pulled on her with all their might. Gradually, she turned in the river and headed for the Atlantic. The rain that began to fall at departure had little effect on the sightseers. She was escorted by countless small craft, including military planes. She had a total of 1,792 passengers on board. There were also 7,000 sacks of mail in the holds that was worth $20,000 to USL. It was estimated that the liner would take in over $520,000 in revenue on the first trip alone.

The flagship of the American Merchant Marine was at last on her way to Europe for the first time in four years. Although she faced stern competition from the Cunard and White Star Lines, Americans finally had a superliner they could be proud of. As with her recent sea trails, the big ship was headline news on both sides of the ocean. There was much speculation about how fast the *Levi* would turn out to be and whether or not she had a chance to take the speed record from the venerable *Mauretania*. Only time could answer the question, however.

The *Levi* passed Sandy Hook just after noon and steamed into clear skies. As was to be expected, there were many important passengers on board. The former head of the US Shipping Board, Albert Lasker, was on the liner at the personal request of President Harding. Lasker had been a major backer of the *Leviathan* during the debate of her proper place in the American Merchant Marine. A number of Congressmen also made the trip. They toured the liner and questioned people from all classes as to the service they were receiving. Vincent Aster was also aboard, he planned to celebrate the birthday of his sister in London and then return on the *Levi*.

Captain Hartley denied that there was any attempt made to set a speed record on the maiden voyage. He stressed to the media that the *Levi* was a 6-day 'boat' with a cruising speed of 23 knots. He said that she had an ample margin of extra power available to make up delays. He likened her to the famous luxury train, 20th Century Limited, which could make a faster schedule than was normally advertised but used this to make up any lost time. Staying on the timetable was more important than any mad dashes of speed that consumed more fuel and disrupted the travel plans of passengers. It was an interesting argument.

The first crossing under the US merchant flag went very well. The weather was good for most of the trip and the liner showed herself to be very stable with no reported bouts of seasickness. The passage was completed in five days, 17 hours and 7 minutes at an average speed of 23.65 knots. She tied up at Southampton at 10.00p.m. on 10 July 1923. The Mayor of the city was on hand to greet the liner.

1923 - Back on the Atlantic

```
QUADRUPLE SCREW, TURBINE STEAMER
             LEVIATHAN
       "THE WORLD'S GREATEST SHIP"

     Captain HERBERT HARTLEY, U.S.N.R., Commanding

Abstract of Log      59,956 Tons         Voyage 40 East

From NEW YORK via CHERBOURG to SOUTHAMPTON, JUNE 12, 1926.
```

DATE	LAT. N.	LONG. W.	MILES	REMARKS
				Departure Ambrose Lt.-V., 3:12 p.m., June 12th.
June 13	39.58	62.55	503	Fine and clear, smooth sea.
,, 14	40.02	50.31	573	Fine and clear, smooth sea.
,, 15	43.18	38.53	575	Overcast, light rain, r'gh q't'r'g sea.
,, 16	46.56	26.43	560	Partly cloudy, mod. sea, full visibility.
,, 17	49.13	13.16	557	Light haze, overcast, S.W. swell.
		To Cherbourg	457	Arrived Cherbourg, 7:30 a.m., June 18, 1926.
		Total Distance	3225	

Sea Passage, 5 days, 12 hours, 18 minutes.   Average speed, 24.37 knots
                                                  (or 28.06 land miles per hour)

A 1926 log abstract from the *Leviathan*. It shows an impressive run of 24.37 knots for the USL flagship. (Author's collection)

Above A postcard view of *Leviathan* at Southampton. (Author's collection)

```
QUADRUPLE SCREW, TURBINE STEAMER
             LEVIATHAN
       "THE WORLD'S GREATEST SHIP"

         Commodore H. A. Cunningham

                59,956 Tons

Abstract of Log                          Voyage 2 East

From NEW YORK via CHERBOURG to SOUTHAMPTON, MAY 4, 1929
```

DATE	LAT. N.	LONG. W.	MILES	REMARKS
				Departure Ambrose, 5:38 p.m., May 4, 1929
May 5	40.06	64.47	416	Moderate Southerly breeze
,, 6	40.00	52.25	568	Gentle Easterly breeze
,, 7	42.37	41.18	552	Light variable breeze
,, 8	46.29	29.10	568	Light Westerly breeze
,, 9	49.08	15.24	577	Gentle SW'ly breeze
		To Cherbourg	541	Arrived Cherbourg 9:09 a.m., May 10, 1929
		Total Distance	3222	

Sea Passage: 5 days, 10 hours, 31 minutes
Average Speed: 24.68 knots per hour

On the eastbound portion of Voyage 2 under Chapman ownership the *Levi* chalks up an impressive run of nearly 24.7 knots. (Author's collection)

Right An excerpt from a tourist cabin Log. (Author's collection)

TOURIST CABIN LOG

ONCE AROUND THE DECK
By G. EDWARD PENDRAY

The bursting white crests of the waves cut by the prow....three old ladies beyond the Second Class rail trying to keep covered up with one blanket....members of Allen White's Orchestra taking themselves seriously....two lovers who have known each other exactly ten hours....the middle-aged lady who is addicted to the psuedo-western novels of Zane Grey....the pretty girl in green with alluring lips and icy eyes....the young man on the top deck who reads economics constantly, with never a look at the sea or the girls....the boy with the radiograms, and the people who are always getting them....

The young man who has tried for three days to borrow a match, seemingly without success....the group of middle-aged men sitting near the windy stairs on the starboard side, for reasons of their own....the long, straight green path in the wake of the ship, stretching clear back to New York, maybe....engaged girls sighing for fiances they left in the States....blatant Californians who want everyone to know they have lived in Los Angeles....the young couple who politely but firmly insisted on having their own deck chairs....the sullen growl of the steering engine underfoot....

Four young girls leaning over the side, deciding for themselves whether the foam made by the ship looks most like mottled green marble or soapsuds upon the bluing water in an agitated washtub....children playing shuffleboard with amazingly poor aim....the color of the sea being compared to everything from emeralds to soup....the talkative middle-aged man who flirted with every girl on the boat....the old lady explaining how she avoided sea-sickness on her last voyage....the elderly persons on the port side of D deck who refused to move their chairs so the young folks might dance....and the bursting white crests of the waves cut by the prow.

How to Get Into An Upper Berth

1—Tie towel around head for protective purposes.
2—Tie towels around feet for same purposes.
3—Close eyes and count six to the sway of the ship.
4—On the sixth count grab the first handle that can be reached.
5—Leap nimbly toward berth.
6—Restrain castigatory remarks as much as possible. Remember there may be ladies in the next cabin.
7—Untangle head and other parts of anatomy from plumbing apparatus.
8—Repeat in homeopathic doses as required.
9—If you have not succeeded in getting into berth by six o'clock, remove padding and dress for breakfast.
10—At breakfast do not forget to remark: "My deah, you have no ideah how mahvelously I slept lahst night!"
G. E. P.

It's peculiar how a girl will syndicate her affections when she is on board a ship.

Jeff, I'm a Mutt

When the wind blows warm and the moon shines clear, and you're out at sea with no one near (that matters), well, wouldn't you? Its a funny thing about the ocean, its disturbing influences to the finer emotions, its own little way of making one feel that freedom of the seas in our very being. That is, perhaps, responsible for the following story:

When a certain charming young lady in the Tourist Cabin, came on her trip to Europe, leaving behind her the boy of her dreams, who answers to the name of Jeff, promising to write him immediately she was tempted by some flirtatious male, but as we said before, the ocean is responsible for a lot.

One evening she was tempted many times and made several appointments, but being late for the first, she tried to make the others, but was interrupted by No. 1 by whom explanations were expected.

The last we saw of her she was on her way to the writing room, saying "Jeff, I'm a mutt, I should have written you in the first place."

This is usually the result of her boy friend having put her back in circulation.

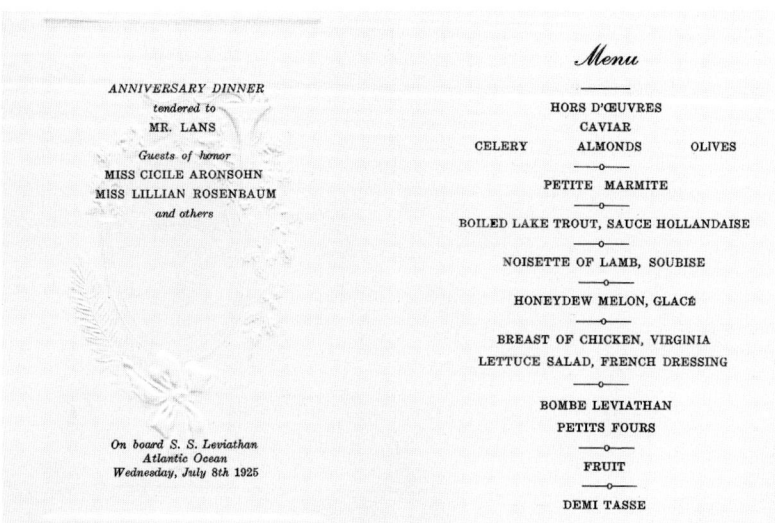

An 'Anniversary Dinner' menu aboard the *Levi* in 1925. (Author's collection)

This log abstract from 1925 shows a very slow crossing of only about 19.5 knots. It must have been a very rough crossing! (Author's collection)

The return phase was even more successful from the standpoint of speed. The *Leviathan* arrived at New York on 23 July after completing the crossing at 23.9 knots. She had taken 5 days, 12 hours and 11 minutes to cross the Atlantic. Over 8,000 people were there to cheer the ship and her 1,259 passengers. Ten stowaways had been discovered and a dog and a cat had wondered aboard at Southampton. The cat was named Levi and the dog Nathan. This was a play on the liner's nickname 'Levi-Nathan' given to her during the war. Notable passengers that disembarked included August Keller, the head of the Ritz-Carlton Hotel, Senator David Walsh of Massachusetts, Reginald Vanderbilt, banker George Reynolds, artist Howard Christy and comedian Al Jolson. US Lines proudly announced a gross profit of nearly $380,000 on the first voyage. The future looked promising.

The *Leviathan* quickly settled into a regular pattern of crossings. She would make a round trip (voyage) every three weeks. The ship would leave New York on a Saturday and arrive at Southampton on a Friday after a brief stop at Cherbourg. After a four-day turnaround, she would then depart Southampton on a Tuesday, pick up additional passengers at the French port and return home by Monday. About five days was allotted at New York to prepare the liner for a new voyage. The turnaround itself required a tremendous amount of work. The *Levi* had to be meticulously cleaned and new supplies, including fuel, taken on board. There was a busy schedule of maintenance to be carried out. Obviously the whole affair had to be organised to the smallest detail.

The year 1923 would be an interesting one for the *Leviathan*. It seemed that she made news constantly. In August she and the *Olympic* left New York at the same time and a 'race' was reported. The *Levi* completed the crossing in 5 days, 11 hours and 16 minutes. She beat the *Olympic* by over fourteen hours. In October another incident with the same White Star liner took place. In a rough storm, *Olympic* overtook the *Levi* and deliberately blew soot all over her from her funnels. The *Levi* accelerated, caught up with *Olympic* and returned the favour.

The speed of the *Levi* in 1923 did not disappoint the ship's fans. On 14 September, she arrived at Cherbourg after averaging 24.81 knots for the crossing. This would turn out to be the fastest trip of her career although she made many crossings over 24 knots. In November the *Levi* grabbed more headlines when she made a 'record' westbound crossing of 5 days, 7 hours and 20 minutes between Cherbourg and the Ambrose Lightship. This beat the speed champion *Mauretania*'s best time between the two points by 13 minutes. She had made daily runs of 402, 617, 605, 614, 593 and 247 miles. The total distance traveled

Top, far right A USL ad highlights the magnificent Social Hall of the *Levi*. (Author's collection)

Top, right and centre An ad for USL under Chapman operation. (Author's collection)

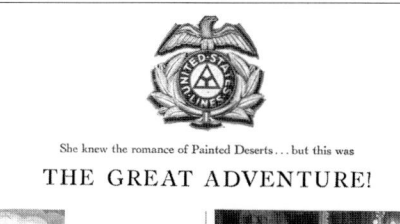

Below The engine room layout of the *Leviathan*. (US Library of Congress)

Right A US government ad for the *Leviathan*. (Author's collection)

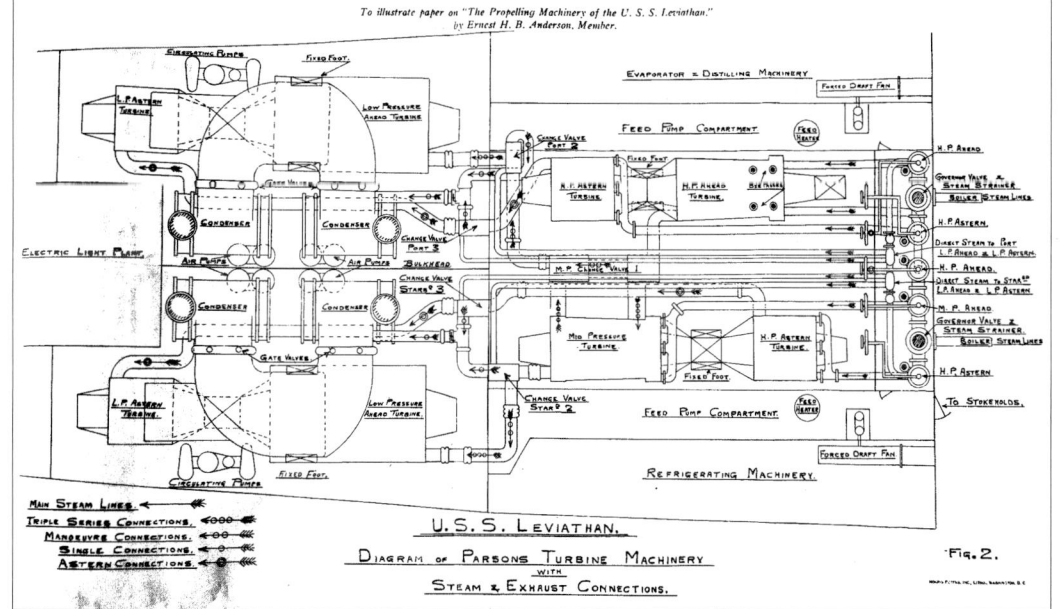

A Leviathan Miscellany

This period postcard of the *Leviathan* at New York offers an impressive night view of the liner. (Author's collection)

Above A colourful view of the S.S. George Washington. (Author's collection)

Right Leviathan Christmas card.

In this photograph a small whiff of smoke is visible coming from the *Leviathan*'s dummy smokestack. (Steamship Historical Society of America)

A colour postcard image of the *President Harding*. (Author's collection)

The SS *America* (ex-*Amerika*) in a period colour postcard. (Author's collection)

A colour postcard image of the *George Washington*. (Author's collection)

A colour postcard view of *Republic*. (Author's collection)

The USL houseflag while under government ownership. (Author's collection)

An excellent colour postcard view of the *Levi*. (Author's collection)

A colour postcard image of the *Leviathan*. (Author's collection)

The main social hall. (Author's collection)

The impressive pool. (Author's collection)

The main dining room. (Author's collection)

The first class children's playroom. The facilities look pretty stark by today's standards. (Author's collection)

The smoking room from a period brochure. (Author's collection)

A first class suite. (Author's collection)

A first class suite. (Author's collection)

An atmospheric view of the *Levi* at her home port. (Steamship Historical Society of America)

Above This computer generated image of the *Leviathan* gives a good impression of the USL flagship in colour. (Paul Wright)

Below This cutaway was typical of ocean liner advertisements of the time. (Author's collection)

Left A colour postcard image of the *Leviathan*. (Author's collection)

Below Cunard's *Mauretania* was the fastest ocean liner in the world from 1907–1929. (Author's collection)

Above This splendid drawing of the *Leviathan* was used in brochures. (Author's collection)

Right A USL advertisement for the *Leviathan*. As was usual for the time, the size of the tugs is understated to focus attention on the star of the image: the *Levi*. (Author's collection)

Interesting Facts about the LEVIATHAN

The largest ship in the World.
Gross tonnage, 59,956.65 tons.
Reconditioned at cost of $8,500,000.
Length over all 950′ 7″.
Breadth 100 feet.
Normal horse power 66,000.
Maximum horse power 100,000.
Quadruple screw, turbine engines.
Originally built as the German S. S. Vaterland and commissioned in 1914.
Passenger accommodations

First Class	*976*
Second Class	*548*
Third Class	*1878*
	3402

20,000 square yards of carpet.
3,000 square yards Oriental Rugs.
15 miles of piping for plumbing fixtures.
500 miles of electric wiring.
15,000 electric lamps.
600 telephones.
72,000 pieces flat and hollow silverware.
120,000 pieces chinaware.
48,000 pieces of glassware.
76 lifeboats, totalling 4,750 person capacity.

United States Lines
General Offices: 45 Broadway, N. Y.
Managing Operators for
U. S. SHIPPING BOARD

PRINTED IN U. S. A.
U. S. 943

The back cover of 'The Press Hails the *Leviathan*' brochure. (Author's collection)

The front cover of 'The Press Hails the *Leviathan*' brochure. (Author's collection)

The COMMANDER
Captain Herbert Hartley

BORN in Oswego Falls, N. Y., in 1875, Captain Herbert Hartley early developed a love of the sea largely influenced through his reading of books devoted to ships and the stirring adventures of men who followed nautical careers. After finishing his preliminary schooling, the young man determined to start off on a seafaring career. This was not altogether agreeable to his father, and when he determined to become a cadet on the frigate Saratoga, loaned by the United States Navy Department to the State of Pennsylvania as a training ship, he expended five dollars of his meagre savings to induce an elderly acquaintance to pose as his father and give the necessary permission for his enlistment. During his two years service aboard the Saratoga, young Hartley visited many of the world's most interesting ports, and was taught seamanship by two young officers then rating as ensigns, but who later came into prominence during the world war as high officers. These two men were Admiral William S. Sims and Captain William H. Fletcher.

Following his graduation with high honors at the age of twenty, young Hartley entered the service of the American Line as a cadet—this was in 1895, and he continued steadfastly with that line until his recent appointment to the command of the Leviathan.

During his service as a cadet, young Hartley was a member of the crews of the St. Paul, St. Louis, Philadelphia, New York and Kroonland. The greater part of his career however, was spent aboard the S. S. St. Louis. In this connection it might be pointed out that Captain Hartley's sea service is unique in the annals of American Merchant Marine history in that he was with the vessel from the time of her launching until he attained to the command, a post he retained up and through the stirring days of the war.

During the World War, the St. Louis, renamed the Louisville, was active in transport service. As commander of the Louisville, Captain Hartley earned for himself many honors including the navy cross, for exceptional devotion to duty, and bravery. Following the war, Captain Hartley commanded various vessels.

When the word was brought to Captain Hartley that he had been chosen commander of the Leviathan, he was silent for a time, and then remarked to a group of friends: "This will make Emily happy." Emily, the guiding spirit of Captain Hartley's life is his fourteen-year-old and motherless daughter.

When Captain Hartley was recently asked as to whether or not he had a hobby, he replied that he had two, one his daughter Emily, and the other, books. This statement succinctly sums up the personality of the Leviathan commander. It is a personality that will endear him to the thousands of travelers who will this summer cross the Atlantic on the greatest steamship in the world.

A biography of Captain Hartley from 'The Press Hails the *Leviathan*' brochure. (Author's collection)

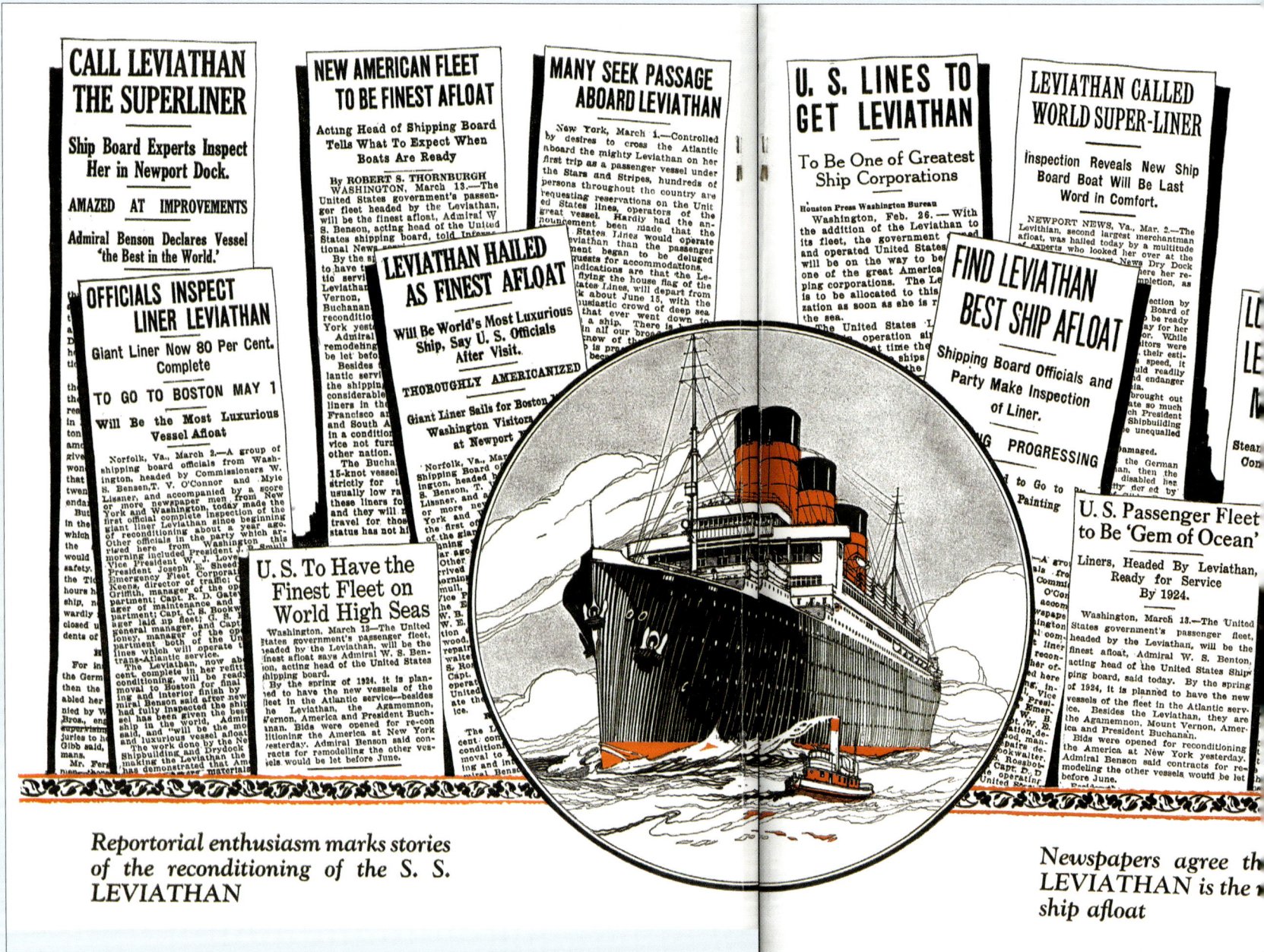

The inside of 'The Press Hails the *Leviathan*' brochure. (Author's collection)

Above and left These postcards highlight the impressive appearance of the *Leviathan*. (Author's collection)

Right This cheerful ad invites Southampton residents to tour the giant vessel on her first trip to Southampton as the USL flagship. (Author's collection)

Left A colourful ad for *Leviathan*. (Author's collection)

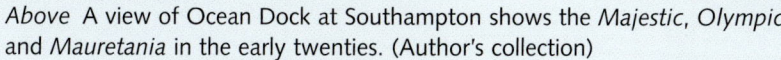

Above A view of Ocean Dock at Southampton shows the *Majestic*, *Olympic* and *Mauretania* in the early twenties. (Author's collection)

Below The *Levi* at New York. (Author's collection)

Above A USL ad from the Chapman era. (Author's collection)

Right The cover of a tourist cabin log from 1926. (Author's collection)

Above In this colourised view of Southampton Docks the *Leviathan*'s funnels are painted in the colours of the old American Line. *Olympic* and *Mauretania* are also present-with the correct funnel colours. (Author's collection)

Above An early artist's conception of the *America* of 1940. (Author's collection)

Left USL tag with the *Levi* on it. (Author's collection)

Left The cover of a brochure from the period of Chapman ownership. (Author's collection)

Right The logo used by the Chapman company. (Author's collection)

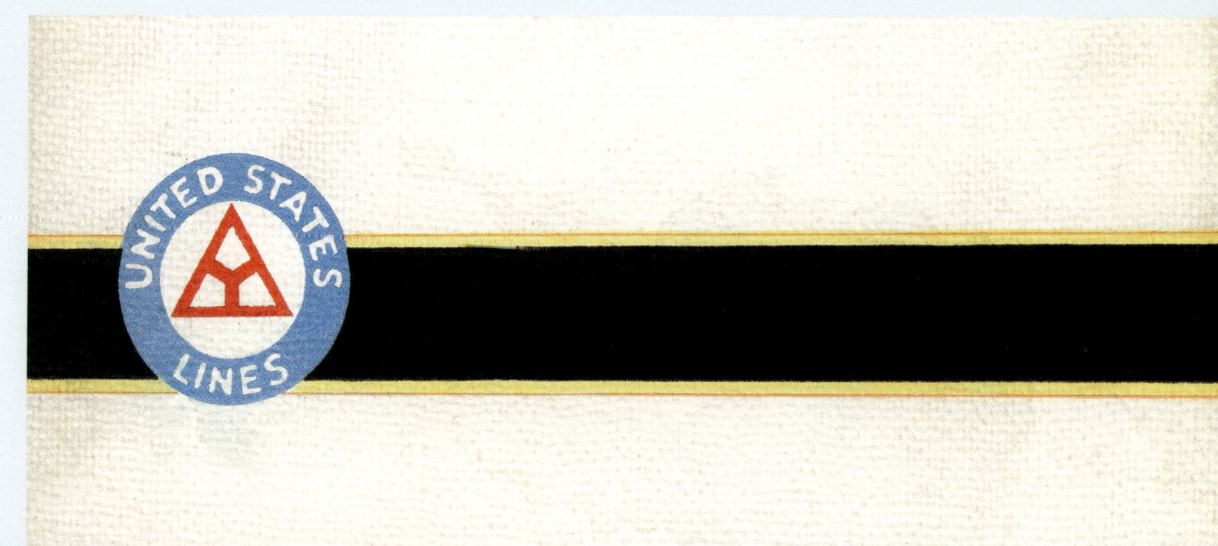

Above The IMM logo for USL. (Author's collection)

Right The cover of an IMM brochure from the thirties. (Author's collection)

The arrival of the ultra-modern French Liner SS *Normandie* in 1935 signalled to many that the days of ships of the *Leviathan*'s generation were numbered. (Author's collection)

The *Levi* in a period postcard. (Jim Holmes collection)

Above A postcard view of Cunard White Star's *Queen Mary* of 1936. With a cruising speed of 28½ knots she was the fastest liner in the world from 1938-1952. She was a very successful liner and was finally retired in 1967. The *QM* survives today as a floating hotel and museum in Long Beach, California. (Author's collection)

Right The *Mauretania* in her final days in the mid-thirties. She was painted white in 1933 for extended cruising service. (Author's collection)

Above The *America* of 1940 had a long and successful career for several owners. She was eventually wrecked while under tow in 1994 and was declared a total loss. She served as the prototype for the much larger and faster SS *United States* that debuted 12 years later. (Francis Palmer-Dave Boone collection)

Left The SS *United States* would emerge as the true successor to the *Leviathan* in 1952. She too, unfortunately, would suffer a premature retirement like her predecessor when she was abruptly withdrawn from service in 1969. (Photo courtesy of Nicholas Landiak and the SS *United States* Conservancy Archive Project)

This Chapman era ad grossly exaggerates the *Leviathan*'s size in comparison to the tug. This was very common in liner advertising of the period. (Author's collection)

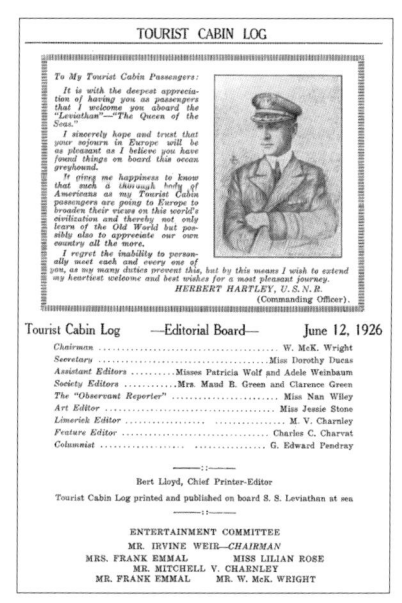

Page 2 of the tourist cabin log from 1926. A message from Commodore Hartley greets passengers. (Author's collection)

Page 3 has a message from Commodore Hartley. (Author's collection)

Page 4 from the 1926 Tourist Cabin Souvenir Log. (Author's collection)

Page 5 from the 1926 Tourist Cabin Souvenir Log. (Author's collection)

had been 3,078 miles. She had averaged 24.17 knots. Although this trip did qualify as a record, the *Levi* did not arrive at New York with a blue ribbon nailed to the masthead. Officially, the *Mauretania* still held that prize with a 1909 crossing of the Atlantic at 26.06 knots between Daunts Rock and Ambrose. This was the starting point for gauging crossing time on Liverpool to New York voyages (the Liverpool route was shorter by about 300 miles.) The best time the *Majestic* had recorded for a westbound journey to date was 5 days, 12 hours and 18 minutes. The 'Magic-Stick' had also averaged 24.76 knots on an eastbound trip. The *Levi* had a 0.05 knot edge on her sister from the September voyage in the same direction. With some justification, the *Leviathan* could claim to be the second fastest liner in the world. It was quite an achievement.

She set other records as well. Her first calendar year of service with USL proved she was a popular vessel. In sixteen crossings she averaged 1,122 passengers per trip, making her one of the most successful liners of her day. Her sister *Berengaria* had carried 1,031 per crossing that year and the *Majestic* 1,268. The *Leviathan* had held her own against the established competition. She was the second most patronised liner on the Atlantic. There was much to be proud of.

Profits also seemed to flow to USL from the *Leviathan*, at least at first. The company claimed that she made a little over $100,000 after expenses in 1923. This was most likely a gross profit, however, not a net profit. Gross profit factored in only the direct operating costs of the ship while net profit subtracted overhead and depreciation charges as well. Figures released later indicated she suffered a loss of about $71,000 in 1923. Other reports claimed a loss of nearly $1,000,000 in her first full year of USL operations. It was all very confusing.

The *Levi* continued to carry many notable passengers, from politicians to movie stars to athletes. A crossing to New York completed on 13 October saw the following people of interest aboard: Congressman Porter and Senator Ladd, swimmer H.F. Sullivan, Arctic explorer Dr Stefansson, actresses Cissy Loftus and Nora Bayes, authors John T. Burke, Florence O'Neil and Herbert Corey, Judge Pendleton, a group of naval aviators who had won the prestigious Snyder Cup, and former Ambassador Loomis.

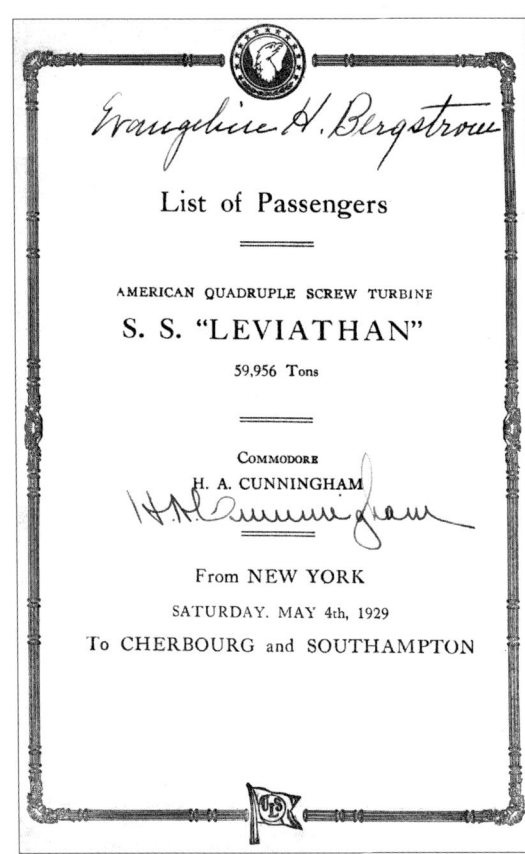

Commodore Cunningham signed this 1929 passenger list for the *Leviathan*. (Author's collection)

The *Levi* was not immune from technical problems. The gremlin struck on the eastbound portion of voyage six on 21 October 1923. The port astern turbine began making strange noises. Eventually the liner was forced to stop while the problem was evaluated. The ship proceeded on three screws for a time and then only two when more problems developed. The engineering team gradually nursed the turbines back to health over the next few days and with all shafts restored to operation, the *Leviathan* worked back up to nearly 24 knots by the last day of the crossing. The problem with the astern turbines that dated back to the ship's early days obviously had not been remedied by the refurbishment.

The *Leviathan* hosted a Christmas party for 300 children of Southampton on 12 December 1923. They were treated to a dinner and given a tour of the ship. Santa Claus, of course, made an appearance in the Social Hall and presented gifts to the children. Many liners provided this type of charity to kids when schedules permitted.

The year 1923 would end on something of a sour note for the *Levi*. On 21 December, she approached New York on the completion of voyage eight, her last for the year. At around 10.30a.m., passengers noticed that something was wrong – the liner had stopped. She had run aground near the lighthouse off St George. Fog may have played a role in the incident. The *Levi* had gotten too close to the lighthouse even though its siren was sounding. Strong current also could have made the situation worse. The ship took on a noticeable list, she

Above Fares for USL in 1927. (Author's collection)

Left A 1927 sailing schedule for USL. (Author's collection)

1923 – Back on the Atlantic   97

Right The cover of the 1927 USL Sailing Schedule. (Author's collection)

drew 35ft of water at the bow and 41ft at the stern. When it became obvious that the liner was not going anywhere soon, tugs were called for to help free her. With 830 passengers aboard and over 6,500 bags of holiday mail in the holds, it was also decided to remove most of the passengers by tugs and ferry boats. Once high tide reached the stranded liner, twenty tugs finally pulled her free after six hours in the mud. The *Levi* then proceeded to Pier 86 and docked around 8p.m. Inspections revealed no hull damage from the accident.

With the damage to the astern turbines two months earlier, USL announced that the *Leviathan* would be withdrawn from service for repairs and normal maintenance. The work was expected to take two months. About 1,000,000 blades would have to be replaced in both the port and starboard low-pressure turbines. She would also be dry docked in Boston for her regular hull cleaning. Her next crossing was scheduled to begin on 22 March 1924.

It had been quite a year for the *Leviathan*. Although not all the publicity had been positive, overall Americans seemed proud of their ship. She had proven herself to be a reliable and comfortable vessel. Her popularity was bound to increase over time. At long last, the United States had a superliner. The future seemed bright.

Below The *Levi* enters the Boston drydock in 1923. (Author's collection)

A diary entry from a 1929 crossing on the *Leviathan*. (Author's collection)

The *Leviathan* air-mail experiment. (Steamship Historical Society of America)

Above Sisters at Southampton: *Majestic* and *Levi*. (Les Streater collection)

Left The *Leviathan* is freshened up in drydock for the season. (Steamship Historical Society of America)

seven

The Roaring Twenties

The year 1924 was to be another eventful one for the *Levi*. In some ways it would be one of bad luck, with technical difficulties forcing her out of service and to dry dock more than once. Her popularity would also slip slightly compared to 1923. She was the fourth most popular liner that year; with the *Majestic*, *Aquitania* and *Berengaria* ahead of her. But as usual, she remained a ship that made headlines and was known worldwide as the flagship of the US merchant marine.

The turbine repairs and other work in dry dock took longer than expected and the *Leviathan* did not return to service until 12 April 1924. She took out a respectful load of 957 passengers. Over 5,000 people gathered to view her departure. Captain Hartley and Thomas Rossbottom, a manager of US Lines, boasted that the ship was in superb condition and that a new aide to navigation – a new type of Sperry gyroscope – had been installed on the bridge. The captain urged Americans to sail aboard the *Levi* and said that she 'reflected credit to our country.'

She carried many interesting passengers that year. Cardinal Hayes returned from Europe aboard her. USL prepared a special altar for him in the Social Hall. The famous movie star couple Douglas Fairbanks and Mary Pickford also crossed in her. Nine-year-old movie star Jackie Coogan, perhaps best known today for his role as Uncle Fester in the 1960s TV series *The Addams Family*, sailed in the USL flagship on a sightseeing trip to Europe. He was photographed in several different locations on the liner. General Pershing, who had traveled aboard the *Levi* during the War, also made a voyage on her. Nearly sixty boy scouts and four of their leaders crossed in July, they were on their way to Copenhagen for the annual World Scout competition. The Chicago White Sox and New York Giants baseball teams chose the *Leviathan* as their means of return to the US after a series of exhibition games.

Perhaps the most unusual passenger of 1924 was not a person at all, but a giant baseball. It had started its journey in Chicago earlier in the year and had been rolled through more than thirty cities in nine states by boy scouts as a publicity stunt to attract new members. Twenty-seven mayors and nine governors had signed the ball.

Still smarting from her defeat in the 'race' the year before, the White Star liner *Olympic* beat the *Levi* on a summer crossing in 1924. Both ships left New York at the same time and the *Olympic* recorded a higher average speed for the trip than her rival, 22.7 compared to 22.64 for the *Levi*. It was sweet revenge for the British vessel.

A run of bad luck for the *Levi* began in August on a westbound crossing. On the sixth, a day out of Southampton, a shudder passed through the ship and she listed to port. Captain Hartley made his way to the bridge and immediately ordered the speed to be reduced. It was soon obvious that she had lost a propeller blade. Number two shaft (inboard starboard position) had to be shut down and locked to prevent further damage. Unfortunately, this not only deprived the liner of shaft horsepower, but the useless screw also acted as a brake. Barely ten hours later ill luck again caught up with the *Levi* when she lost another blade on shaft four (the screws were numbered 1–4, starting with the starboard shaft). Only 286 miles were covered that day. Nonetheless, she still worked up to 19 knots the next day with only two shafts working normally. Despite the trouble, the *Leviathan* completed the trip in 6 days, 21 hours and 19 minutes with an average speed of 18.8 knots.

Arriving at New York a day late, the ship quickly proceeded to the Boston dry dock. The damaged screws were repaired and some minor hull work completed. It was also found that propeller number three had a cracked blade. This was welded as a quick fix and the incident was later attributed to a faulty propeller design. She left the dock on 15 August and, after a very rapid turnaround, departed for her next voyage on schedule the next day. However, this was not to be the end of her technical gremlins and she lost another blade on 20 September. The *Levi* once again went into dry dock. Inspections revealed that the shaft was also damaged. The next crossing was delayed until 4 October.

As 1924 came to a close, the *Levi* had a very rough crossing. On the return leg to New York during the week of Thanksgiving the big ship ran into a storm with winds of up to 100mph and waves approaching 60ft in height. Eleven portholes were smashed and several people injured, none seriously. The *Levi* covered only a few miles in one day when the gale blew her around as if she were a sailing vessel. To keep her on course it was necessary to hold the wheel hard to port and she listed twenty degrees in the same direction for some time. After the wind subsided somewhat, a heavy fog surrounded the ship. But the Atlantic had more to throw at the *Levi*: a heavy snowstorm with bumpy seas. The ship arrived a day late at Pier 86 with a crossing speed of only 19.47 knots.

The *Levi*, her annual overhaul just completed, left New York on her first voyage of 1925 on 28 February. There were only 596 passengers aboard – not the best way to start the new year. It was, however, the off season and large passenger lists were the exception at that time of the year. Notables on board included the wife and daughter of New York Governor Alfred Smith and Congressman H.W. Watson. Captain Hartley also had the honour of presiding over the marriage ceremony of actress Nora Bayes to Benjamin Friedland. It was only her fifth marriage. On her return in April, Bayes said that her new husband had purchased her home and then given it to her as a gift so no one would say he was living in his wife's house.

There was also a 'cat crisis' aboard the *Leviathan* in 1925. A report spread that 292 cats were thrown overboard. Since many sailors were a superstitious lot who believed that a ship without cats was in for bad luck, the story had some traction in the media. It was later revealed that while over fifty stray cats were rounded up on the crossing and put into 'lock-up', most were taken back by their owners and some were put ashore at Southampton. Cats were very common on passenger and cargo vessels. They kept down the rodent population and were frequently adopted by crew members. On the *Leviathan* it was not uncommon to see cats napping on the lifeboat covers on a sunny day.

Several other events sparked interest in the USL flagship that year. Passengers and crew witnessed a small battle between a coast guard vessel and a 'rum runner' while the *Levi* was anchored off of Quarantine one night. Machine-gun fire was directed at the belligerent ship in the darkness. Captain Hartley said both ships appeared only briefly and that he thought the rum runner got away. A first class passenger also had $7,000 worth of jewelry stolen. During the trip another act of thievery took place when author Constance Drexel caught someone stealing from her purse when she returned to her cabin. The crook fled and was later identified by the writer in a line up. All this happened on a single crossing in October.

One of the most famous people to walk the decks of the *Leviathan* in 1926 was Queen Marie of Rumania. She left quite an impression on the passengers and crew. She boarded the liner at Cherbourg on 12 October bound for the states at the cost of the US government. She travelled with her son and daughter, 17 other personnel and 160 trunks. With the Rumanian flag flying on her mast, the officers and crew of the *Levi* gave her a royal welcome. They stood at attention as she came aboard. American warships were close by. The Queen immediately asked to see the pool, which she had heard much about. Her suite had been painstakingly prepared by USL to please her in every way. The bed covers were made of Russian lace and the pillows had the Rumanian Royal Crest on them. The rooms that made up the suite were filled with flowers. The galley also was ready with some of the Queen's favorite foods. The chef even created a new dish named in her honor.

On her second day on board the American flagship she got up early and swam in the pool. Breakfast was served on her private sun deck. The Queen's daughter and son explored the ship, with the prince being shown around the bridge by Captain Hartley. The Queen also read on deck and socialised with passengers. She signed autographs and knitted caps for herself. She was an instant hit with her audience, described as being informal and charming.

The *Leviathan* completed the crossing, which was front page news across the world, at an average speed of 23.93 knots. The 3,092 miles was covered in five days, nine hours and ten minutes. It was voyage 45

The Roaring Twenties   101

The Club *Leviathan* is the centerpiece of this Chapman era ad. (Author's collection)

A USL advertisement for the *Levi*. (Author's collection)

An ad for the launching of the SS *America* in 1939. (Author's collection)

An ad for USL under IMM ownership. (Author's collection)

An IMM advertisement from *National Geographic* magazine. (Author's collection)

west for the *Levi*. The weather was relatively good for most of the trip. The Queen departed at Quarantine for an extensive series of formal receptions and diplomatic functions.

The *Leviathan* would build on her successes the next few years. Her popularity increased every year from 1925–1927. In 1926 and 1927 she was the number one liner on the Atlantic with an average of 1,300 passengers and 1,448 per crossing, respectively. The *Majestic* was not far behind her with 1,219 per trip in 1926 and 1,304 the next year. Overall passenger carryings broke the 1,000,000 mark in 1927 for the first time since before the First World War. The numbers would increase again for the next two years before falling rapidly after the Great Depression seized the world in its iron grip.

As the *Leviathan's* passenger figures rose, so did her revenues. The *Levi* finally began to earn a more consistent gross profit on an annual basis. She was in the black by nearly $1,000,000 in fiscal year 1926. She would soon be at her peak and was approaching the long elusive goal of turning a net profit.

One of the most exciting events of 1927 involved an airplane flight off of her deck. This was a time when airplanes were still relatively new and there were many aviators vying with each other to break the next record and push the technological envelope a little bit further. Aviator Clarence Chamberlain proposed to USL an experiment in which he would take off in his plane from the *Levi* and then land back in the states. The offer was accepted and an 80ft-long wooden launching platform was built over the *Leviathan's* bridge. On 1 August 1927, the liner departed New York. Several naval vessels accompanied her. The big event took place 2 August. The *Levi* turned into the wind and accelerated to 24 knots. At 8.14a.m., Chamberlain's aircraft successfully lifted off the hastily prepared runway and took to the sky. After a quick circling of the *Levi* to impress her passengers, he headed for land and touched down at Curtis Field at 10.25a.m. The distance traveled had been about 67 miles. A sack of mail from the *Leviathan* was also delivered by Chamberlain to post office personnel after he landed; the first time such a feat had been accomplished by a passenger liner. The whole affair generated much talk of a 'ship-to-shore' service in the future that would expedite the movement of mail, and perhaps some passengers willing to pay an extra fee, from ocean liners to their destinations. The amount of publicity produced by the flight was no doubt highly pleasing to the leaders of USL. The *Leviathan* had been front page news for days.

One of the biggest events of 1928 was the passing of the Merchant Marine Act by Congress. Government support was provided to private ship owners to help offset higher labor and building costs in the US when compared to foreign lines. It established construction loans of 75 per cent of the cost of a new ship at an interest rate of 3.5 per cent over a 20-year period; a mail subsidy for US passenger vessels; and an insurance program. A rebirth of the US Merchant Marine was in the works. Another major episode for the year was the sudden departure of Captain Hartley. He resigned in January before the *Levi* had returned to service for the new season. Captain Harold Cunningham was appointed his successor. Hartley went to work for the proposed Blue Ribbon Line. This new company planned to build ten liners that could cruise at over thirty knots and would use airplanes to complete the trip for high priority passengers and mail. In the end, however, the whole plan fell apart and the ships were never built.

After a slight drop in passenger numbers in 1928, the *Leviathan* was on the rebound in 1929. She was most likely operating at a net profit at this point and was proving to be a valuable asset to the US Merchant Marine. Her very existence was a grand advertisement for all American passenger and cargo vessels. She had earned her title as the 'World's Greatest Ship.' After years of uncertainty, the Shipping Board finally decided to sell USL to a private operator. The winning bidder was announced as P.W. Chapman & Company Inc. Ownership was transferred on 21 March 1929.

The *Levi* was officially handed over to the new company on 8 April in a ceremony attended by over 300 guests. A new houseflag was raised on the aft mast, white with a star and a triangle on it. A check for $4,000,000 had been presented to the US Shipping Board as the first installment of the $16,000,000 owed for the eleven vessels purchased. USL almost immediately cut 100 people from the *Levi's* crew, taking it below 1000 and another 200 people were laid off from other vessels. Chapman officials called the American liners 'overstaffed' when questioned about it. The contract required USL to operate the *Leviathan* for at least 13 voyages per year for 10 years or pay a hefty penalty of $150,000 per cancelled voyage. The new owners announced plans to build two superliners in the 40,000 ton range to run with the *Levi* and two intermediate ships of around 30,000 tons each. The list for the new Chapman fleet recorded the USL vessels in order by size: *Leviathan, George Washington, America, Republic, President Roosevelt* and

President Harding. Another five ships were listed under the American Merchant Lines banner.

The *Leviathan* began voyage 1 (the now privately owned USL started the voyage numbers all over again) under her new owners on 10 April. Just over 900 passengers were aboard. The ship returned with a much healthier load of 1,177. The *Levi* set a record on her departure from Cherbourg on a westbound crossing on 29 August. She had 2,716 passengers on board – the most of any liner since before the war. From June to October 1929 she was the number one liner in overall passengers carried. The management of USL was very pleased and scheduled more trips for the liner to bring in more revenue. Her 1928 program of 30 crossings was boosted to a planned 33 for 1929. The extra voyages would occur during December when many other ships were out of service for their annual overhauls.

The *Leviathan* once again took place in a test involving an airplane in 1929. She was selected to carry the patented Adams Air Mail Pick-Up System. The device was attached to the Poop Deck and leaned over the side of the ship about 100ft above the water. A bag of mail was attached to the end of it. USL, seeing a huge opportunity for publicity for their flagship, did all they could to promote the event. Special stationary was printed and thousands of airmail envelopes were brought aboard for the event. A reporter was even given free passage in one of the Imperial Suites. It was hoped that, if the device proved practical, it would reduce the delivery time of mail by sea by about two days.

On 25 May, the *Leviathan* departed New York at 11.30a.m. with 1,610 passengers on board. She arrived at Cherbourg on 31 May after a crossing of five days and twelve hours with an average speed of 24.15 knots. After a quick turnaround at Southampton, the *Levi* headed westward on 2 June with 957 passengers. There was much excitement as the big day approached. The liner slowed to 21 knots as she approached the Grand Banks on 7 June. It was expected that the pick-up would take place when the *Leviathan* was about 300 miles off the coast. Unfortunately, as with many groundbreaking endeavours, the experiment failed. The first plane that took off from New Jersey quickly crashed, thankfully without loss of life. The second plane got lost and was struck by lightning. A third failed on 8 June because the *Levi* was not informed of it and when the plane showed up there was no mail on the pick-up system.

It was decided to attempt the pick-up again on the next eastbound crossing of the *Leviathan*. She left on 12 June at 3.30p.m. with an impressive load of 2,132 passengers. When she was sixty miles out and passing Fire Island, a Fairchild Monoplane swooped down and dropped a sack of mail on the Poop Deck. The plane then returned and picked up the outgoing bag of mail. The *Leviathan* now had another feat to add to her list of firsts – the successful pick up and delivery of mail at sea. Unfortunately, the Adams system would prove to be unreliable in the long term and USL lost interest in the concept.

But the year would end on an unhappy note. The *Leviathan* pulled out of Pier 86 for voyage 13 on 7 December 1929. Although the crossing represented yet another technology breakthrough that was pioneered by the *Leviathan*, the establishment of the first regular telephone service between ships and land, it would soon be overshadowed by a hidden structural weakness in the design of the vessel. Late in the day on 11 December, the *Levi* was battling mountainous seas. The ship was taking a tremendous pounding. Ropes had been strung in the public rooms and corridors to assist people who actually tried to move about the ship during the gale. At one point, the bow rose nearly into the air and then slammed into the Atlantic. A sound like a gun being fired spread throughout the ship. The ship had cracked. The hull had opened for about 20ft, extending from C to D-deck on the starboard side. The crack was a few inches wide at some points. Rivets had been sheared off and it was possible to look through the crack and see the ocean. Luckily, the fracture was well above the waterline. Some bulkheads were also warped, making it almost impossible to open some cabin doors. The forecastle deck had collapsed almost 4in. The wave had carried away several lifeboats. An investigation later determined that several design flaws related to the expansion joints, split uptakes and shell plating that was too thin, along with the stresses of the storm, had contributed to the accident. The *Majestic* had suffered a similar crack five years earlier.

The *Leviathan* was patched up at Southampton, under the supervision of the British Board of Trade, with a dozen steel girders. Her planned departure on 16 December was postponed while the work was carried out. She left Southampton the next day with over 1,200 passengers aboard. British officials had ordered the ship to use the longer southern route to return home to reduce the stresses on the weakened hull plates. The liner arrived at New York a day later than normal, after encountering thick fog and snow on Christmas Eve.

The repair work would consume about three months. Nearly 6,000 rivets were driven into the structure and 76 steel plates installed.

Dozens of cabins and lavatories had to be removed to make way for the effort. It was a huge task that required a special hydraulic riveter that was developed specifically for the Leviathan's problem.

The Leviathan would also undergo a thorough refurbishment while the crack was mended. The arrangement of the lifeboats on A-deck was changed from six sets of three nested boats at each station on both sides of the deck, to eight sets of two boats each. The boats on the forecastle were also reduced and later removed altogether. The passenger capacity was adjusted to 940 in first class, 666 in second class and 1,402 in third class for a total capacity of 3,008. The ship also went into dry dock as was usual for her winter lay-up.

Virtually the entire passenger accommodation was overhauled and updated. The change that received the most publicity was the opening of the 'Club Leviathan'. It replaced the Palm Court and was basically a night club at sea. It was very modern in design and must have seemed quite out of place to some in a ship decorated in period styling. The lighting was indirect and could be adjusted in intensity and colour. The colours used in the room were brown, orange, blue and gold. The ceiling was light blue and mimicked the sky. A carpet with black musical notes woven into it was a central feature. The dance floor was circular and covered in linoleum and a special orchestra was hired just for the club. 'Talking pictures' could be shown as well when the screen was uncovered and chairs placed on the dancing floor. Along with the nearly unchanged Ritz Carlton restaurant that connected to it, the Club Leviathan was 100ft long and 55ft wide. It became one of the most popular of the ship's many fine public rooms. The cost of the renovation was over $500,000.

Right This computer rendering shows the approximate location of the crack the Levi suffered in December 1929. (Adapted from an image by Paul Wright)

Right The Art Deco-styled Club *Leviathan*. (Author's collection)

Left The Club *Leviathan* added during her overhaul after the crack in December 1929. Its modern style contrasted sharply with the period décor used in the rest of the liner. (Author's collection)

eight

The Long Twilight

The 1930s was defined by the economic disaster of the Great Depression. It all began in October 1929 when the stock market crashed. By the end of the year investors had lost over $15,000,000,000 and the US economy began to slip into a recession. Although there were some signs of recovery in 1930, the situation worsened considerably in 1931. The worldwide economy seemed to collapse as nation after nation plunged into economic chaos.

The ocean liner trade was not immune to the downturn. Although the overall passenger numbers in 1930 remained just above 1,000,000, down only about 6 per cent from 1929, this represented only the beginning. The year 1931 saw the numbers drop 30 per cent to under 700,000. In 1934, only 460,000 people crossed the Atlantic. This represented a catastrophic dip of nearly 55 per cent in the number of passengers carried from 1930. Although the amount of crossings conducted by liners was also reduced dramatically during the early 1930s, there were still too many ships in service for the business available. It was a very hard time to be in the transatlantic passenger trade.

To make matters even worse, a new generation of liners was entering service in the years before and during the Depression. During much of the 1920s, the pre-war ships had been adequate to meet the demand. The ex-Ballin trio had led the pack until 1929. But their dominance was coming to an end. No less than seven new superliners were built between 1927 and 1936. The *Ile de France* of 1927 was the first. Although strictly conventional from an engineering standpoint, her interiors were very modern and represented a break with the past tradition of period-style decoration. In 1929 North German Lloyd unveiled the 51,656 ton superliner *Bremen*. She was fitted with the latest in marine technology. Her geared turbines generated up to 130,000hp and could push her to more than 27 knots. She captured the Blue Riband from the *Mauretania* on her maiden voyage when she crossed the Atlantic in 4 days, 17 hours and 42 minutes at an average speed of 27.83 knots. Her superstructure and funnels were streamlined to reduce air resistance. She also had a bulbous bow below the waterline, it projected ahead of the ship and reduced fuel consumption by up to 5 per cent. Her engines and boilers were much more efficient and powerful than those on the *Leviathan*. The *Levi*'s power plant weighed 227lb per nominal horsepower while the *Bremen*'s was 159 – a saving of 30 per cent over the American ship. The *Bremen* had twenty boilers while the *Levi* had forty-six; the German liner burned less fuel, about 830 tons a day, than the *Levi*'s 950, but had a cruising speed several knots faster than the American vessel. She consumed 0.7lb of fuel per shaft horsepower per hour, while the *Leviathan* burned nearly 1lb of fuel using the same system of measurement.

The *Bremen* also surpassed the *Leviathan* in her interior design, embracing the Art Deco movement of the late 1920s. Gone was the dark, carefully carved wood panelling that was the trademark of Victorian architecture. It was replaced with more simple accommodations that made use of streamlined and geometric shapes, vibrant colors, lacquered wood, plastic and glass and indirect lighting to create an atmosphere that appealed to the new decorative tastes

With the *Leviathan* the first of the Ballin trio to be withdrawn, the *Berengaria* carries on the tradition at the 1935 Fleet Review at Southampton. (Author's collection)

In her final full year of service, *Olympic* (sistership to the ill-fated *Titanic* and *Britannic*) leaves Southampton for New York in August 1934. She now flies the dual flags of Cunard and White Star following the merger earlier that year. (Author's collection)

Above White Star's *Homeric*, the former NDL liner *Columbus*, was part of White Star's express service and proved a poplar cruise ship in her latter years. (Author's collection)

Left In the Boston Drydock at night. (Steamship Historical Society of America)

of the 1930s. The *Leviathan* seemed old and outdated by comparison. The *Bremen* quickly became the most popular liner in service.

With the competition increasing, and the number of available passengers decreasing, the *Leviathan* returned to the Atlantic on 12 April 1930. General Pershing was among the 570 passengers. First class bookings fell sharply in the first few months of the year. For the first time since 1924, the *Levi* would average less than 1,000 passengers per trip in 1930, 863 to be exact. She was down almost 25 per cent from the year before. Unfortunately, the situation would go from bad to worse over the next few years.

1931 was another difficult year for the *Levi* with bookings dropping 28 per cent from 1930. The liner began to slip into the red as her revenues declined. The same thing was also happening to scores of liners on the Atlantic. Many ships were offering cruises between transatlantic crossings to bolster earnings. The *Leviathan* made her first cruise in July 1931. It was a four-day voyage to Halifax, Nova Scotia and back. Although the cruise lost money, it was still cheaper to run the cruise than lay up the ship. The Chapman Company also began to have financial problems and it defaulted on its payments to the

Right An officer aboard the *Leviathan*. (Steamship Historical Society of America)

A rare view of the *Manhattan*. (Author's collection)

Below The *Manhattan* passes the laid-up *Leviathan* in the 1930s. (Steamship Historical Society of America)

The *Levi* at New York in her final years. (Author's collection)

Three sisters at Southampton in July 1930. *Leviathan*, *Majestic* and *Berengaria* make a grand trio at the British port. Who could have imagined before the First World War that the former *Vaterland*, *Bismarck* and *Imperator* would one day be operated by three competing lines? (Les Streater collection)

This page The *Levi* in Bremerhaven in her twilight years. (Author's collection)

The *Washington* of 1933 would serve her country for nearly 20 years in peace and war. (Author's collection)

The *Levi* glides into the Boston Drydock in November 1930. (Author's collection)

Shipping Board. The *George Washington*, *America* and *Republic* were repossessed by the board and laid-up. Rumors of a possible sale of USL to IMMCO began to circulate. The International Mercantile Marine Company was back in the picture again.

Commodore Cunningham retired in January and was replaced by Captain Randall. The transfer of command ceremony was relatively simple. On one of the bridge wings Commodore Cunningham handed Captain Randall the ship's papers and good luck wishes were exchanged. The new commander's parrot, Barnacle Bill, amused onlookers with his noises and comments. Captain Randall would go on to become one of the most popular skippers the *Leviathan* ever had.

With the Depression biting deep, the two superliners that had been conceived to run with the *Leviathan* were quickly cancelled. However, plans for two intermediate liners called for in the sales contract to Chapman went ahead. The New York Shipbuilding Corporation had been selected in May 1930 to build the ships. The keel for the first liner, yard number 405, had been laid on 6 December 1930 in Camden, New Jersey. Construction on the second vessel began on 30 January 1931. These liners were the largest ever built in America at the time. They emerged in 1932 and 1933 as the *Manhattan* and *Washington*, respectively.

With the financial condition worsening, USL began to look at ways to cut costs. With the stroke of a pen, the *Leviathan* lost her dubious claim as the largest ship in the world. Her tonnage was 're-measured' as 48,590 gross and 15,801 net tons (down from 59,957 and 27,696 tons in the same order). Since port charges were based on tonnage, USL said this would save about $40,000 annually. The ship's advertising slogan was modified from 'World's Greatest Ship' to 'America's Greatest Ship.' Obviously the company no longer saw value in advertising their superliner as the largest, it was simply no longer worth the money.

On 10 December 1931 the *Leviathan* was once again transferred to new owners. IMM had won the bidding process for USL. The revised contract required the line to run the *Levi* for a minimum of seven voyages per year through 1936 or pay a $10,000 fine for each trip not conducted. A modified version of the old American Line houseflag, with a blue eagle and the initials USL on it, was raised on her mast. It was the *Levi*'s third owner in less than three years. The *Leviathan* departed for Cherbourg and Southampton on 12 December with a mere 312 on board, not an encouraging sign for the new company.

The circumstances did not improve in 1932. The *Levi* averaged 6 per cent less passengers per crossing than the previous year. This was a drop of 48 per cent from her 1929 numbers. The other big ships were also suffering. The *Olympic* averaged only 430 per crossing, the *Majestic* 531 and *Aquitania* 656 that year. USL also modified her itinerary in 1932 to include an extension to Hamburg. For the first time since 1914, the former *Vaterland* returned to her birthplace. Unfortunately, the new service proved to be a disappointment. The number of passengers exchanged at Hamburg was not enough to justify the extra time and expense of going to Germany. Her departure point at New York was also moved from Pier 86 to the IMM docks at Pier 59 in May 1932.

For USL, however, there was reason for optimism. On 11 August 1932 the new *Manhattan* left New York on her maiden voyage to Hamburg via Cobh, Plymouth and Le Havre. She carried an impressive 856 passengers on the eastward crossing and 1,108 on the return trip. She was 705ft long and 86ft wide. Her gross tonnage was over 29,500. She had twin screws driven by geared turbines. The service speed was 20½ knots and she turned out to be a very economical vessel to operate, consuming only about 222 tons of fuel per day on her first twenty crossings. She was an instant hit with the traveling public. Her superb performance convinced USL management that the future of transatlantic travel was in the medium-sized liner. They quickly reached a momentous decision – the *Leviathan* had to go.

Normally the *Levi* sat out the winter off-season, especially during the lean years of the Depression. However, USL requested that the Shipping Board allow them to operate the liner for seven additional voyages in 1932–1933. The company claimed that the ship was vital to the future of the merchant marine and should not be laid up as usual while foreign vessels remained in service. Jobs would also be preserved by running her during the winter. Although this seemed to be a great gesture by USL in favour of the long-term operation of the *Leviathan*, later events put the whole affair in a different light. If she was losing money on peak-season trips, how could she possibly turn a profit in the bleak winter months? It is likely that USL planned to use the off-season crossings as ammunition to the Shipping Board to grant permission to retire a ship that was losing more money then ever before.

When the predictably low passenger loads became a reality, USL made its move (an October 1932 crossing had only 125 passengers aboard). A request was made to the Shipping Board to retire the

The final dry-docking of the *Leviathan* in 1934. (Author's collection)

Leviathan. In return, USL would promise to begin construction of a new liner, larger and faster than the *Manhattan* and *Washington*, to replace the *Levi*. The company claimed it had lost over $560,000 on the *Leviathan*'s voyages since December 1931 (about $250,000 less then had been predicted). The ship that had been vital to the US Merchant Marine only months earlier was now declared obsolete by her owners and ready for the scrap pile. The *Levi*'s defenders countered that USL had a contract that fully anticipated that the ship would run at a deficit. The Shipping Board had reduced the interest rate on the payments due to it for the purchase of USL by IMM by about $5,000,000 to help subsidise the *Levi*'s operation. Now the board was being asked to subsidise a ship that was no longer operating. The liner had made an average loss of about $5,000 per trip under control of the US Shipping Board from 1924–1929. Although she had been in the red overall the *Leviathan* must have run at a gross profit for some time, and even at a net profit in the late 1920s, under government operation in order for the average loss to be that small. Under Chapman management, the ship had made a gross profit of over $70,000 per voyage. The *Leviathan* had lost nearly $51,000 per trip under IMMCO up to that point. USL argued that the money saved by laying up the *Leviathan* would be used to help pay for her replacement.

To the shock of many, the Shipping Board approved the request of US Lines on 6 May 1933. Permission was granted to cancel the future sailings of the ship and the penalty charges for not operating the *Levi* were waived. USL said that it was the perfect time to withdraw the *Levi* from service since the new *Washington* was nearly ready to join the fleet. The news was radioed to the liner when she was a day out of Hamburg. She had 254 passengers on board and the announcement was greeted with disbelief and sadness. A farewell dinner was held for Commodore Randall. He was slated to take command of the *Manhattan* after the withdrawal of the *Leviathan*. The *Levi* arrived at her berth on 12 May. With only a small crew aboard to perform minimal maintenance, it seemed that her day was over. Many predicted that her next trip would be to the ship breakers. In October she was moved to a familiar location – Pier 4 at Hoboken – where she had docked as the *Vaterland* nearly two decades earlier.

But the story was not yet over. The ship's fans refused to accept the situation. After a year of pressure, the Shipping Board ordered USL to return the *Leviathan* to service in 1934 and fulfill their contract for seven voyages that year. Although the company could have refused and paid the $70,000 in penalty costs, USL chose to follow the wishes of the board. It took 16 days, and approximately 1,500 gallons of paint, to spruce up the ship after her long lay-up. The liner was dry docked and carefully inspected. USL spent $150,000 readying the *Levi* for her return to the sea. With Commodore Randall once again on her bridge, the *Leviathan* pulled out of Pier 59 on 9 June 1934 with a respectable load of 551 passengers. The impossible had happened – the *Levi* was back.

The excitement was to be short-lived, however. USL decided to only operate the liner for five voyages in 1934 and pay the fine of $10,000 each for the two trips they would not undertake per the contract requirements. Although the *Leviathan* did better than the *Majestic* in average passenger per crossing that year, 519 apposed to 499, she continued to run at a loss. The *Berengaria*, meanwhile, had beaten her sisters with 541 per trip and the *Manhattan* had carried 664 per crossing that year. This further convinced USL management that superliners were no longer viable. The year 1934 was the worst in thirty years for transatlantic travel, with only about 460,000 choosing to cross the 'Great Pond'. The company claimed deficits on the liner of about $120,000 per round trip for the year. The *Leviathan* was not alone in this category. The *Majestic* lost approximately $86,000 and the *Berengaria* $76,000 on each voyage. These losses were widely circulated in the press and served the political interests of the line by allowing them to claim the *Levi* was hopelessly outdated and ready for retirement. It was even suggested that the operation of the ship in 1934 had delayed plans for her replacement. Ultimately, it was cheaper for USL to pay the relatively small fine to the government rather than operate the *Leviathan*. The *Levi* arrived home on 14 September and was once again withdrawn from service. Commodore Randall returned to the *Manhattan*. The events of over a year earlier were repeated as the great liner was abandoned and moved back to Pier 4 at Hoboken. But this time there would be no reprieve.

Officials of USL made it quite clear that they had no intention to ever operate the *Leviathan* again. They said they would pay the $70,000 fine for each of the next two years. The five-year contract expired after that point. The company asked the Shipping Board for permission to place the *Leviathan* on the government retired list. The board agreed and the ship faded from the spotlight.

In the meantime, plans for a replacement vessel moved slowly ahead. The ship would at last appear in 1940 as the 33,532-ton *America*. She was 723ft long and 94ft wide. With a cruising speed of over 22 knots, she was a superb liner, one of the finest ever to fly the stars and stripes. She would remain afloat for over fifty years. But she was no *Leviathan*. It would not be until 1952 that the US would have a superliner of the *Leviathan*'s calibre. The SS *United States* filled that void when she streaked across the ocean that year and easily captured the transatlantic speed record for her country.

As she awaited her fate at Hoboken, many of her competitors were making their final journeys. The *Mauretania* and *Olympic* sailed to the scrappers in 1935 as victims of the merger between Cunard and White Star. The *Homeric* followed in 1936; the *Majestic* was sold for demolition the same year, but was saved at the last minute and converted into the naval training vessel HMS *Caledonia*.

But there were occasional newsworthy items about the old liner. In 1937 there was serious talk about turning the *Levi* into a training vessel. Others called for using her as a floating hotel for the World's Fair in 1939. Negotiations also took place to move the ship to Puerto Rico to serve as a hotel there. Another possibility was that the ship would be held in reserve with the *George Washington* and *America* for use as a troop transport in the event of war. In August of the same year it was reported that the US Maritime Commission, the successor

The Long Twilight 113

Above This rare image, probably taken in 1933, shows the *Leviathan* and *Majestic* together (center) at Pier 59 at New York. It should be obvious to the observer why they were considered sisterships. (Bill Miller collection)

Left This 1934 ad announced the return to service of the *Levi* after a one year lay-up. Unfortunately, her come back to the Atlantic would be short-lived. (Author's collection)

to the Shipping Board, would allow USL to trade in the liner to the government as a $2,000,000 down payment on a replacement vessel. All the talk, however, remained just that and the *Levi* continued her sad lay-up at Hoboken.

The *Leviathan* was again a ship of big headlines on 1 October 1937, though the news was not good. '*Leviathan* Doomed, New Ship Ordered' shouted a headline in the *New York Times*. USL called for bids from ship breaking firms. The situation was settled by December when the liner was sold for $732,000 to a consortium of British scrapping companies. A British crew of about 150 men were assembled and sent to Hoboken in early January 1938. Retired White Star Captain John Binks, once a master of the *Olympic*, arrived on the *Berengaria* to command the final voyage of the *Leviathan*. He had also commanded the *Caledonia*, ex-*Majestic*, on her last trip from Southampton to her new berth as a training ship at Rosyth in 1937. His statement to the press is worthy of repeating here:

> I am not exactly sentimental about the *Leviathan* being broken up because I know ships of her type do not pay these days, with such vessels as the *Normandie* and *Queen Mary* and other new ships. But I do feel sad to realize their day is gone, because my day has gone, too.

As with everything surrounding the *Leviathan*, drama was not far behind. A labour disagreement delayed the scheduled departure by two days. For a time it was uncertain when she would leave for Rosyth, Scotland. Finally, On 25 January 1938 the ship began to slowly back out of her slip at 4.37p.m. It had been raining for some time, but the sky cleared and a rainbow appeared shortly before the last sailing. To some, the rainbow appeared to end at the *Levi*. Smoke was pouring from her two working funnels and mud swirled as the propellers forced her out of the sludge that did not seem to want to let her go. Aside from her rust-stained hull and superstructure, she looked odd with her trimmed funnels and masts. This had been necessary in order for her to pass under the Firth of Forth Bridge near the scrapyard at Rosyth. It took half an hour for the tugs to manoeuvre her out of Pier 4. Under the gaze of onlookers, including former Captain Harold Cunningham, she quietly turned into the river at 5.10p.m. Cunningham remained silent as his old command left his sight forever. His eyes seemed fixed on the *Levi*. The sun had nearly disappeared on the horizon and the *Leviathan* stood out as a dark silhouette, with a sprinkling of lights here and there, against the New York skyline. It was not hard to imagine her in her heyday as the queen of the seas. Many refused to allow her departure to go unnoticed and a small fleet of boats appeared as an escort. Then the ship gave two blasts from her whistle, followed by a long, sombre one that echoed across the harbour. The small craft around her responded in kind. It was a moving moment for those present. The *Levi* anchored until 2.00a.m. off Pier 8 to take aboard more fuel. She was then forced to wait for the high tide four hours later. She was delayed yet again when a medical kit was sent out to the ship by tugboat when it was discovered the ship did not have one. Thousands of people took advantage of the late departure and came to the waterfront to catch a last glimpse of the grand old liner. With the final preparations completed, the *Leviathan* raised anchor and steamed away from her adopted country, never to return.

The crossing was a rough one. Years of deferred maintenance had taken a toll and the ship's powerplant was temperamental on the trip. Things did not get off to a good start when the stem anchor chain broke and the anchor plunged to the bottom of the Atlantic. More problems followed: a worker in the engine room fell off a ladder and broke his jaw; the hot water would not work properly; the food was unsatisfying; the cabins were filthy and there was a lack of bed sheets and pillowcases; the crew was undisciplined and lethargic; dust filled the air; the quartermaster frequently steered the ship off course; several small fires broke out; the ship's boilers proved troublesome; the steering system malfunctioned and at one point the ship came to a stop; the ship leaked; and there was an intense snowstorm and fog to contend with. One of the strangest moments of the trip was on 1 February when a short circuit caused the ship's siren to blow unexpectedly across the empty ocean. It was an eerie reminder of the time twenty years earlier when a similar event happened on a crossing with troops on board. It seemed as if the liner was mourning her impending demise. But the 'excitement' was far from over.

After a voyage of 3,164 miles at an average speed of 17.1 knots, the *Leviathan* let go her anchors off the Scottish coast on 3 February 1938 and waited for favorable tides so she could make her way into the dockyard. The wait would be a long one – eleven days. The crew began to pack since their work was done, or so they thought. Suddenly, a ferocious windstorm descended on the ship and drove her towards the rocks at Haystack Island. Steam pressure had been allowed to subside and the ship was almost helpless. Her anchors provided little assistance. Only after the quick acting engineers diverted all possible power to the engines was the *Levi* able to control herself and move away from the treacherous rocks. It had been a close call.

On 12 February it appeared that the liner was ready to complete the final leg of her journey. But bad weather again reared its head and forced her to wait another day. The *Leviathan* later drifted too close to shore and ran aground. Tugs had to be summoned to free her. Another attempt failed the next day when an oil pipe ruptured and engine power was lost.

But the *Levi* had exhausted her last delaying tactic. On 14 February all the elements finally came together. The *Levi* gently passed under the giant Firth of Forth Railroad Bridge and slipped through the locks into the docking area at Rosyth. Once she was made fast to the wharf, the number one hold was flooded so she would settle into the mud. This was a precaution to prevent the wind from blowing her around during the demolition process. Her propellers slowed to a stop. Her whistles let out three last gasps. For the final time, the command 'finished with engines' was telegraphed to the engine room. The end had been reached.

After the auction of her passenger fittings in March, the actual breaking up could begin. The sale netted over $65,000 and over 5,700 lots were offered. The items sold included furniture, wood panelling, carpet, eating utensils and virtually anything that could not be melted down in the furnaces of the shipbreakers. Many took advantage of the opportunity to take home a souvenir of the historic vessel.

Ironically, the *Leviathan* was scrapped in the site of her sistership *Caledonia* (formerly *Majestic*). The naval trainees aboard the former White Star liner had a good view as the torches gradually reduced the once pride of the American merchant fleet to scrap. Much of the steel from the *Levi* would be used for ammunition in the upcoming Second World War. The *Berengaria* and *Caledonia*, however, would not outlast their sister by very long. After a series of fires made her safe operation questionable without a costly overhaul, Cunard sent the *Berengaria* to the breakers' yard in December 1938. After the start of the war, the *Caledonia* was moved to a different site for protection against possible air attack. Plans were discussed to use the ship as a troop transport, but fate had other ideas. The former *Majestic* was gutted by fire on 29 September 1939 and was declared a total loss. Her remains were quickly sold for scrap.

In 1939, with the space she was occupying needed for other vessels, the cut down hull of the *Leviathan* was towed out of the docks and driven ashore. On 14 February 1940, with the Second World War in full swing, the last remnants of the proud ship were hauled off the beach. Over 38,000 tons of high grade steel had been salvaged from the ship. Although the metal was of great value, it paled in comparison to the service the *Leviathan* could have provided as a troop carrier during the conflict. She had the capability to carry over 14,000 troops in a single trip. But the shortsightedness of officials in the US ended any such possibility. Why was it acceptable to scrap a liner of the *Levi*'s potential when smaller ships such as the *George Washington* and *America* (1905) were held in reserve by the government? Both vessels would serve admirably in the war. It is difficult to understand why the *Leviathan* was allowed to be demolished while less capable vessels were retained; a satisfactory answer has never been provided.

And so ends the tale of the *Leviathan*. Her career was one of great successes and heartbreaking failures. But perhaps that is why she was so admired in her day. Had things been just a little different, she might have served her country during the Second World War and survived into the late 1940s. History is full of such 'what ifs', but in the end it does not matter. The *Leviathan* left behind a rich legacy and her triumphs far outweighed her shortcomings. Despite the fact that she had no compatible running mates, could not serve alcohol as freely as foreign vessels, was operated by a government agency for much of her career, had higher crew costs under the American flag and faced intense competition on nearly all fronts, she was one of the most popular liners of the 1920s. For two of those years she was the top liner on the Atlantic, yet there are people even today that describe the *Leviathan* as unpopular and unprofitable during her years as a USL ship. However, there are many who take exception to this and they are in the right on this issue. Americans were rightly proud of their flagship, despite her German origins. She was a household name across the nation, made headlines all her life and earned her place in the record books as a ship of many firsts. She made history in ways most ships never did. Although it seemed that she never did anything the easy way, are the truly important things in life ever easy?

In the final analysis, she was more than just a collection of metal parts. She was the *Leviathan* – America's First Superliner. What else needs to be said?

With her masts and stacks trimmed so she can fit under the Firth of Forth bridge at Rosyth, the *Leviathan* awaits her final voyage from New York to the breakers' yard. (Charles Dragonette collection)

Final call: The *Leviathan* arrives at the scrapyards at Rosyth on 14 February 1938. The Naval Training Vessel HMS *Caledonia*, ex-*Majestic*, is docked to the right. The two sisterships were reunited in their final days. (Jim Duckworth collection)

Appendix I

Vaterland/Leviathan Passenger Carrying Statistics

Contrary to what some believe, the *Leviathan* was a very popular liner. She was very competitive with her sisters *Berengaria* and *Majestic*. In her first year of post-war service she was the second most popular liner in Atlantic service; *Majestic* was ahead and the *Berengaria* in third place. In 1926 and 1927, the *Levi* was the number one liner in terms of average passengers per crossing. From 1923–1932, the *Majestic* was typically the most popular of the Ballin trio with the *Levi* and *Berengaria* not far behind. The *Aquitania* and *Olympic* also did very well – but not to the extent of the *Imperator* Class. They were extraordinarily successful liners.

Year	Number of Crossings	Total Passengers Carried	Average per Crossing
1914	7	16,850	2,407
1923	16	17,959	1,122
1924	24	23,600	983
1925	28	30,523	1,090
1926	28	36,387	1,300
1927	28	40,539	1,448
1928	30	33,529	1,1i8
1929	32	36,311	1,135
1930	27	23,303	863
1931	29	18,116	625
1932	22	12,960	589
1933	8	2,048	256
1934	10	5,190	519

Career Total: 289 crossings (144.5 voyages)
Total Number of passengers carried: 297,315
Average per crossing: 1029
Average per crossing in the 1920s: 1,171
Average per crossing in the 1930s: 570

Sources

Transatlantic Passenger Conference Reports.
Leviathan: The World's Greatest Ship, by Frank Braynard.

Special Note: These figures are primarily from records of the Transatlantic Passenger Conference. They may not always agree with other sources since the number of voyages a ship made in a year was sometimes rounded if the number of crossings was not even. This was mainly due to the fact that the liner might be at sea when the calendar year changed. However, this should have only a minimal effect on the averages.

Appendix II

1925/1929/1934 Passenger Statistics Comparison

The following compares the performance of the top five liners on the Atlantic in 1925/1929 and the top fifteen in 1934 in terms of average passenger load per crossing. As can be seen, the combined effects of the Great Depression and the arrival of more modern tonnage took a toll on the popularity of the *Leviathan*. By 1934, the top six liners were five years of age or less.

1925

Liner	Number of Crossings	Total Passengers Carried	Average per Crossing
1. *Majestic*	24	28,630	1,193
2. *Berengaria*	31	35,292	1,138
3. *Leviathan*	28	30,523	1,090
4. *Aquitania*	29	28,215	973
5. *Olympic*	26	22,624	870

1929

Liner	Number of Crossings	Total Passengers Carried	Average per Crossing
1. *Bremen*	14	24,960	1,783
2. *Majestic*	28	34,894	1,246
3. *Berengaria*	30	36,853	1,228
4. *Leviathan*	32	36,311	1,135
5. *Ile de France*	32	33,881	1,059

1934

Liner	Number of Crossings	Average per Crossing
1. *Bremen*	34	858
2. *Europa*	34	793
3. *Manhattan*	26	643
4. *Washington*	26	621
5. *Georgic*	19	616
6. *Britannic*	21	588
7. *Columbus*	18	570
8. *Berengaria*	32	541
9. *Ile de France*	30	519
10. *Leviathan*	10	519
11. *Majestic*	31	499
12. *Aquitania*	27	492
13. *Kungsholm*	13	474
14. *Empress of Britain*	24	454
15. *Gripsholm*	16	447

Sources

Transatlantic Passenger Conference Reports
Leviathan: The World's Greatest Ship, by Frank Braynard.
Majestic: The Magic Stick, by Mark Chirnside

Appendix III

Leviathan Speed Data

The *Leviathan* also did quite well in the speed category. From 1923–1929 it was fair to call her the second fastest passenger vessel in the world. She made many trips at over 24 knots. Although her fastest crossing was 24.81 knots and the *Majestic*'s was 25 knots, the *Levi* would prove to be consistently faster than her sister ship. The arrival of the German speed queen *Bremen* in 1929 made these performances seem less impressive since the German liner took the speed record with a crossing at 27.83 knots. Nonetheless, the *Leviathan* proved to be a fast ship – especially for a type of vessel that was said to be designed only for moderate speed.

Year	Average Speed in Knots
1923	23.00
1924	23.04
1925	23.77
1926	23.33
1927	23.60
1928	23.54
1929	23.60
1931	23.19
1932	22.96
1934	22.94

Note: All years are not available.

Sources

Transatlantic Passenger Conference Reports.
Leviathan: *The World's Greatest Ship*, by Frank Braynard.

Bibliography

Primary Sources
The Cunard Archive, Sydney Jones Library, Liverpool University.
Transatlantic Passenger Conference Reports.

Books
Braynard, Frank. *Classic Ocean Liners Volume 1: Berengaria, Leviathan, and Majestic*, 1990.
Braynard, Frank. *Leviathan: World's Greatest Ship*. Volumes 1–6. Privately printed, 1974–1983.
Braynard, Frank. *S.S. United States – Fastest Ship in the World*. Turner, 2002.
Braynard, Frank. *The Bremen and Europa*. Fort Schuyler, 2005.
Burgess, Douglas. *Seize the Trident*. McGraw Hill, 2005.
Chirnside, Mark. *Majestic: The Magic-Stick*. Tempus, 2006.
Chirnside, Mark. *R.M.S. Olympic: Titanic's Sister*. Tempus, 2004.
Dawson, Philip. *The Liner: Retrospective and Renaissance*. Conway, 2005.
Donzel, Catherine. *Luxury Liners: Life on Board*. Vendome, 2006.
Flayhart, William. *The American Line*. Norton, 2000.
Garzke, William H. and John Woodward. *Titanic Ships, Titanic Disasters*. Society of Naval Architects and Marine Engineers, 2002.
Gibbons, John. *Palaces That Went To Sea*. Nereus, 1990.
Goff, Richard. *The 20th Century*. McGraw Hill, 1994.
Graham, John-Maxtone. *The Only Way to Cross*. Barnes & Noble, 1997. (Reprint)
Griffiths, Denis. *Power of the Great Liners*. PSL, 1990.
Hansen, Clas. *Passenger Liners from Germany 1816–1990*
Harding, Stephen. *Great Liners at War*. Motorbooks, 1997.
Hartley, Herbert. *Home is the Sailor*. Vulcan Press. 1955.
Isherwood, J.H. *Steamers of the Past*. Sea Breezes, 1966.
Kludas, Arnold. *Great Passenger Ships of the World Volume 2*. PSL, 1976.
Layton, Kent. *Atlantic Liners: A Trio of Trios*. Café Press, 2005.
Leviathan History Committee. *History of the USS Leviathan*. 1919.
Miller, William. *Pictorial Encyclopedia of Ocean Liners, 1860–1994*. Dover, 1995.
Mills, Simon. *Hostage to Fortune*. Wordsmith, 2002.
Newell, Gordon. *Ocean Liners of the 20th Century*. Bonanza Books, 1973.
Shaum, John and William Flayhart. *Majesty at Sea: The Four Stackers*. PSL, 1981.
Streater, Les. *Berengaria: Cunard's Happy Ship*. Tempus, 2001.
Warren, Mark. *Distinguished Liners from the Shipbuilder Volume 2*. Blue Riband, 1997.
Wealleans, Anne. *Designing Liners: A History of Interior Design Afloat*. Routledge, 2006.
Williams, David and Richard de Kerbeck. *Damned by Destiny*. Teredo, 1982.
Williams, David. *Liners in Battledress*. Vanwell, 1989.
Wills, Elspeth. *Cunardia*. The Open Agency, 2005.

Periodicals
'The Reconstructed Leviathan'. *Scientific American*, August 1923.
Scientific American. 23 May 1914.
The Propelling Machinery of the U.S.S. Leviathan. Ernest H.B. Anderson. The Society of Naval Architects & Marine Engineers. 1919.
The Story of the Leviathan: The World's Champion Ship and the Significance of Her Entry into the American Merchant Marine. United States Lines, 1923.
The Reconditioned Passenger Liner Leviathan. The Marine Engineer & Naval Architect. August 1923. To Shining Sea: S.S. Manhattan and Washington. Peter Kohler. *Steamboat Bill*. Summer 1992.
White Star Magazine. January 1928.

Newspapers
The *New York Times* Historical Archives.

The *Levi* from the Isle of Wight near Southampton. (Author's collection)

The *Leviathan* steams away from the camera in her twilight years. She would soon fade into history, but her memory lives on. (Author's collection)